BESTSELLER!

How to write fiction that sells

Jennifer Bacia

Book titles visible on spines:
ANGEL OF HONOUR — JENNIFER BACIA
UJARZMIĆ ZŁO
ANGEL of HONOUR — BACIA
SHADOWS OF POWER — BACIA

Contents

Why I Wrote This Book

As someone who thought about writing a novel for a long time and then finally did it to amazing success, I know exactly how you are feeling about facing that first blank page.

My aim with this book is to offer you the confidence, motivation and knowledge that will help you to **start your novel, finish one you have already begun, or evaluate and rewrite a manuscript you have had rejected or that you know needs more work but are unsure what to do to improve it.**

Many published authors have received help somewhere along the line and I am no exception. First came a meeting with the hugely successful American suspense writer, Sidney Sheldon who recognized my passion and gave me great encouragement. Later, a meeting with Colleen McCullough led me to super-agent, Selwa Anthony.

Since my own success, I have taught writing workshops and spoken at numerous writers' festivals and had the pleasure of knowing I have helped other aspiring writers to get published. I can say with certainty that you can learn what you need to know. In this book you will find very practical information, particularly as I closely analyze what worked or didn't work in my own novels. I promise by the time you get to the end of *Bestseller!* you will be itching to start writing!

Author's Note

This book was first published as 'Creating Popular Fiction' by Allen & Unwin, Australia, 1994.

In the following updated pages, rather than get caught up in the complexities of hero/heroine, his/her, I have chosen to use the feminine gender throughout. However, the information given here is every bit as pertinent to aspiring male writers of popular fiction.

In the last decade or so of course, the rise of digital publishing has seen huge changes in the publishing industry. Both established and new authors can now publish their work on numerous digital platforms and by-pass the traditional publishing process entirely. But of course with so many 'indie' published books available, it is more important than ever to ensure that your story has what it takes to gain a readership.

Chapter 1: What Sells?

Giving yourself the best chance

When my first novel, *Indecent Ambition*, (originally titled *Shadows of Power*) was published in Australia by Pan Macmillan it was the first time a leading publishing house had taken the plunge in launching a 'local' popular fiction writer with a major publicity campaign.

Like so many others, I'd had the idea of writing a book in the back of my mind for a long time. In the process of creating my first novel I learnt so much. Some things I actively researched before starting, others came to light as I wrote, still others as I went through the process of selling the finished manuscript.

In this book I want to share some of these lessons and learning experiences with you. By pinpointing some of my own areas of difficulty I hope to provide insights and shortcuts that will help you take that wonderful step from wishful scribbler to successful author.

Somerset Maugham once said: 'There are three rules for writing the novel. Unfortunately, no one knows what they are.'

While creativity cannot be manufactured, there *are* guidelines that can certainly assist any aspiring writer of popular fiction. In this book my aim is to offer you the confidence, encouragement and technical information that can help you to sit down and *finish* your first novel.

Writing a novel is neither as hard nor as easy as you might imagine. But there is only one way to find out if you really do have talent— you must sit down and write. Perhaps you think there is something magical and different about people who become writers. They must all be brilliant, highly educated, lateral thinkers, wizards with words… You couldn't be further from the truth. Writers have emerged from amazingly diverse backgrounds: they were once teachers, housewives, accountants, students, lawyers, itinerant workers, nurses, doctors, sales representatives.

What authors *do* have in common are the qualities of determination, discipline, doggedness, resilience and patience. They made up their minds they were going to write and they let nothing stand in their way. On top of that, if they didn't make it on their first attempt they didn't give up.

My aim is to help take the fear and mystery out of writing your first novel by sharing with you those creative techniques that have worked for me.

When I first started to think seriously about writing, I read a number of articles which seemed to dwell on the terrible odds against being published. Yet I saw no reason to allow any of the statistics or negative information to put me off. After all, I figured, what did I have to lose? As far as I could tell, only my time, and I was prepared to sacrifice that.

The result of my efforts did more than fulfil my dreams. My first novel was bid for by major international publishing houses. It was a Doubleday Book Club choice, a UK lead title, the featured book that receives advertising and prominent shelf space, condensed in *Cosmopolitan* magazine and bought by leading foreign publishers. On top of all that, the film rights were optioned too.

Everything those articles had warned me not to expect with a first book had actually happened to me! It was a wonderful start to a career which continues to bring me immense pleasure and reward.

I don't tell you all this to brag. Rather, I hope you will be encouraged by the description of my own success with a first novel. Until you actually make the effort to sit down and finish a manuscript yourself you'll never know if writing might bring you similar reward and fulfilment.

Know your market: What do readers want from popular fiction?

First and foremost they want a story. If you are contemptuous of the traditional storyline that has a beginning, middle and end, maybe you shouldn't be reading this book. Fiction that sells is all about entertainment. Readers want to escape their everyday normal lives. They want to have adventures, live in different times and countries, and assume other identities so they can experience living the life of an international business tycoon, a master spy, a private investigator, a wealthy heiress or a famous actress. As a writer you can have the fun of playing all these roles and, in the process, entertain yourself. Because it's my firm belief that if *you* don't enjoy what you're writing then your readers won't either.

What type of story should you write?

There are fashions in fiction just as there are in most things. To give yourself the best chance of reaching readers, it helps to analyze what is selling, what markets are already crowded and what types of stories might be on the way out.

Novels can be categorized in many ways but they are generally labelled mainstream or genre fiction by publishers.

Novels which are aimed at the widest possible audience—men, women, young adult—are called mainstream. This broad category deals with most areas of modern life including relationships, careers, coming of age, the search for success and fulfilment. They tend to focus with greater depth on characterization but are not usually experimental. Mainstream writers include people like Jodi Picoult, Tim Winton and James A. Michener.

Genre novels aim at the specific interests of their readers. Into this category fall spy, crime, adventure, suspense, horror, historical, romance, teenage and science fiction, among others. Some major writers started their careers as genre writers then branched out into mainstream fiction.

It's my firmly held opinion that one way to make your task easier is to write the type of book you enjoy reading. For example, if you're an addict of crime or horror fiction then these are the types of stories and writing you will already know a lot about. Being familiar with a genre makes your task as a beginner much easier.

Once you've decided on the type of story you want to write, I think it's essential to spend time reading other successful writers' work. If you are starting any sort of business, wouldn't you do your market research and see how your competitors operated? There's no reason why you shouldn't use the same approach with the business of writing.

Having made your selection of popular novels, read them first for pleasure. The second time round you should be reading with a much more critical eye as you try to analyze 'how the writer did it'. This process involves looking past the surface and examining the inner workings that reveal the writer's craft and skills.

Before I began to write, I read dozens of books that were bestsellers at the time. Pen in hand, I analyzed them in detail.

Here are some suggestions of what to look for:

- **When and how is the lead character introduced into the story**? Page one, page three? In a business meeting or in a tropical hideaway? Running for her life or giving birth?

- **How has the author made clear who is the lead character**? This is usually achieved through description, viewpoint— including inner thoughts of that character—and action.

- **What is the conflict or problem** facing the main character? How soon is that problem introduced? Every popular novel *must* involve the leading character in conflict.

- **Make a list of the setbacks** which the lead character must overcome. These are the complications of the plot.

- **What questions are raised to arouse the reader's curiosity?** Is the main character going to get the inheritance which is rightfully hers? Will she see through her enemies' schemes? This is how suspense is created.

- **How many sub-plots are there? At what point are they introduced?** I suggest you underline text dealing with each sub-plot in a different colored pen or pencil so you can see how the sub-plots develop and how they are woven into the main plot.

- **How are the sub-plots linked to the main plot**? Perhaps the heroine's task in the main plot might be to save her firm, while the sub-plot shows her dealing with the obstacles placed in her path by disgruntled former employees.

- Underline characters' names as they are introduced. Note how much or how little description the author uses.

- **Identify the 'villain'. What drives him or her?** Villains must have their own important goals. This is what leads to conflict with the lead character.

- **What is the purpose of the minor characters?** Do they help the main character solve her problem or create further obstacles? Do they help to reveal more about the main character?

- **Where is the story set?** What is the era? Is the time span of the story important? For example, does the main character have 24 hours to foil the assassination plot or find the bomb?

- **Where and how is the love interest introduced**? Do the couple hit it off at once or are they antagonistic or indifferent to each other?

- What incidents happen in the middle of the story to maintain the interest?

- **How is the final crisis handled**? Is the lead character's life in danger? Is so, how does she escape? Is there a happy ending? Were all the loose ends tied up?

Other points to consider:

- After reading the story once, you will know which characters are on the heroine's side and which aren't. If her enemies are only revealed at the end, note how the writer plants clues to their identities in advance. This is called the **foreshadowing of events**.

- Check that all the questions posed at the beginning of the story have been satisfactorily answered.

By the time you've made a close study of a dozen or more books in your chosen genre, you may find your confidence growing merely as a result of having noted how published authors sometimes get away with some pretty questionable character and plot manipulations! Yet through skill and technique they usually still manage to make their stories entertaining and enjoyable.

On the other hand, you might think they have done such a bad job that you're bound to do better.

Can I make a living from writing?

Be warned: only a handful of writers can live exclusively from their writing. If you want to write without financial pressures, you would do best to keep your day job—at least until your name is established and readers are clamoring for your next book. When the money finally does come in, you will then have the freedom to write without the financial stresses that can so often stifle creativity. Having your books earn money is also a great confidence booster because you know you are writing the sorts of stories that people enjoy. Money and recognition are both well-deserved rewards for what is certainly one of the world's loneliest careers.

But I think you can make things difficult for yourself if you decide to write with an eye on earnings alone. The phenomenal sales of a writer like Stephen King, Hugh Howey, Andy Weir, E.L. James, for example, might inspire you to attempt their styles of fiction in the hope of reaping similar rewards. May I remind you though, of my earlier comments on writing what you most like to read. If you choose a genre you are not familiar with, it will only make your writing task a lot harder.

We all need money to survive of course, but a lot of writers earn very little from their work yet never think for a moment of giving it up. The drive to create is what keeps them at their task. That, and hope. Most writers would agree that it is the joy of self expression coupled with the chance of hitting the big time that makes writing so exciting.

It takes more than money to motivate me to sit alone for hours and fill blank pages. As a writer I love the puzzle, the challenge, the chance to explore parts of myself, to communicate ideas that I feel strongly about, to develop and structure a plot that will intrigue and tantalize my readers. Passion is what drives me: the heady excitement of telling a story I have to tell, of exploring characters I can really feel for and believe in.

The best writing—and therefore that which has the best chance of being published—makes emotional contact with the reader. Before that can happen it is essential that your own emotions be engaged. Your first aim in writing should be to thrill, amuse, excite and intrigue yourself. Only when *you* feel a strong connection to your characters can you hope to arouse similar emotions in your readers.

That's why I suggest you make it easy on yourself. If you really want to enjoy the solitary and difficult task of writing, write the sort of story with which you feel most comfortable.

On the other hand, you also need to make sure that the story you choose to tell is not so intimate and personal that it will appeal to only a limited readership. It's important to find the balance between a plot that engages your emotions enough to make you want to do all the hard work of telling the story and at the same time appeals to as wide an audience as possible.

What are the essential ingredients of popular fiction?

I'm sure many of you can remember how bored you were at school when you were forced to study the 'classics'. Not only did they lack action and pace but they were marked by long, tedious passages of description and difficult, obscure language.

When readers of modern popular fiction pick up a book they have certain expectations. Chiefly, these are:

- A strong plot with a traditional beginning, middle and end which must center on believable motivation and conflict.

- Pace and action.

- A hero or heroine with whom readers can identify.

- Romantic interest.

- Intrigue.

- A happy ending—or a promise of one.

To be successful you have to give readers what they want. Therefore, if you can come up with a story that meets the above guidelines, written as best you can, you've given yourself a very good chance of reaching readers.

Give yourself an edge

The popular fiction market is very competitive, so it helps if you can make your work stand out in some way.

My first novel, *Indecent Ambition* had certain elements that helped to distinguish it from the mass of other manuscripts.

To begin with, I attempted to move away from the 'young and beautiful' stereotype with my heroine, Anthea James. I made her a woman in her late 30s who, while attractive and feminine, is also powerful in areas more usually dominated by men—politics and the media.

As well, she is not exploitative: she does not use men or her feminine wiles to get ahead but succeeds by intelligence and determination. When the novel was written, this type of heroine was still a rarity.

What also made the novel stand out was its focus on such topical events as the Bicentenary, and media and political corruption. Again, this was something different for mass market women's fiction. And it struck a chord, both with the publisher's bidding for the novel and, ultimately, where it counts—with the readers.

Chapter 2: What If...

How an idea becomes a plot

Writers are always being asked, 'Where do you get your ideas?' One well-known author used to joke that he subscribed to an annual publication, available strictly to professional writers, which was full of plot ideas. To his amazement he was occasionally taken seriously!

Well, I'm sorry to tell you there are no short cuts. Most writers would admit that plotting is far from easy. For me, it's the agony before the ecstasy of actually sitting down to write.

But if you want to write a novel for the popular market you'd better make sure you understand the vital importance of plot. Your readers certainly do. They expect a story with a beginning, middle and end.

But let me make an important point right here: **You don't have to know the entire story before you start.**

I hope you will read that sentence again. And again. Writing is a creative art and creativity occurs as much during the process of putting words on paper as in the preliminary thinking process itself.

You may already have tried out half a dozen plot ideas only to have them bog down or run out of steam by page 20 or 30. This is when your initial enthusiasm turns to frustration and despair and you throw away yet another attempt.

Please believe me that this is a normal part of fiction writing. It's happened to me dozens of times. Plotting is difficult. Every honest writer will tell you that. It is not easy no matter how many books you write.

Where do you find ideas? Outside sources

Plotting is the challenge, the wall every writer must scale to reach that wonderful moment when suddenly the heart beats faster because you know *this* idea is going to work—this is the one that is going to see you through to the end.

To put it another way, **creating a plot is about solving problems**. First you face the problem of deciding what area it interests you to write about—and then there are the technical problems of where to start, what to put in, what to leave out, how much dialogue to use, how long the story should be, how it should end and so on.

Let's start by looking at the initial problem—what to write about. And that question authors are always asked: 'Where do you get your ideas?'

Professional writers are always on the lookout for anything that can be turned into a plot. All sorts of things can trigger the idea for a story: an overheard conversation, an anecdote, a poem, a film, a personal experience, a particular interest, a dream, a piece of music, television, other people's books.

Other sources of ideas include all media, scientific journals, biographies, talking to people, visiting certain locales. It helps too to read television and movie guides that précis storylines, as these can sometimes act as a trigger on your subconscious.

My friends get little pleasure out of watching television with me or accompanying me to a movie. That's because I am always trying to sharpen my own plotting skills by trying to guess the endings of books, television shows, or movies. It's a challenging exercise and I suggest you try it some time. If the ending you choose is different from the original, then you've got another story! If it's the same, you're beginning to think like a writer—albeit one with few friends!

I firmly believe that if you're going to have any chance of being a published author you must first be a reader. I read voraciously, but my reading now is different from what it was before I took up writing as a career. These days, reading is as much work as pleasure. I am always on alert, as it were. Whether I am reading newspapers, journals, magazines, novels or non-fiction, I am aware of filtering and storing the myriad of facts and ideas so that my subconscious can work at developing my next plotline.

This isn't to say that you can merely lift some real-life story from a newspaper feature and turn it into a best-seller. These stories make the headlines because of their newsworthy aspects. The general public has already been given the details, so all you would be doing is retelling the same story.

But what these sensational true-life stories *can* do is act as a stimulus to your imagination. Because truth is so often stranger than fiction, you may find yourself musing along tracks you have not previously considered. Thinking like a writer means saying to yourself: 'If *that* can happen in real life, then the possibilities in creating a storyline should be endless.'

Where do you find ideas? Inside operations

Another active way to get ideas is to tap into your creative source with a free-association exercise like 'clustering'. This is a kind of private brainstorming session which spawns a whole range of nonlinear associations from which useful patterns can emerge.

Our mental processes are two-sided. Creative thought originates from the right brain, while the left brain is the logical, critical censor. The technique of clustering offers the chance to find again the freedom of expression we knew as children. It allows us to shrug off our inhibitions about nothing we write being good enough unless it's 'whole and perfect'. In clustering, rather than trying to force out complete and logical thoughts, we use a word or short phrase to stimulate mental free-association.

Try writing down the word 'fear' in the middle of a piece of paper and putting a circle around it. Giving yourself only a minute or two, jot down whatever spontaneous associations arise from this initial stimulus. It's best not to hesitate trying to choose or judge. Just write the words that come to mind so that they radiate from the key word, and circle each of them in turn. For 'fear', you might come up with: night, alone, bridge, tall building, failure, airplanes, age, poverty, and so on. Study what you have written for a moment and, using arrows, link up those associations that seem related. Keep in mind that no one else is going to look at what you are doing.

In her book *Writing the Natural Way* (TarcherPerigree, 1983) Gabriele Lusser Rico explains this technique in detail and states that you will know when to stop clustering and begin writing. As she describes it, you will experience a shift in mental mode characterized by a sudden feeling of satisfaction and certainty when you realize that you have something to write about.

This entails looking at the clusters of words for a few moments until you see something that may trigger a first sentence. The profusion of choices you have on the page in front of you should make it easy for you to follow that initial sentence with another and another. What is happening at this stage is an oscillation between right and left brain function—you are using rules of grammar as you write your sentence, then falling back into the creative state as you choose your next impression.

Continue writing for about eight minutes, then end your piece with a sentence that links up with the opening one by repeating a word or phrase or emotion. This gives the exercise a sense of unity.

The next step is to read aloud what you have written and spend a minute or so making improvements where you think they are needed. Finally, you should rework the whole piece for a few minutes until you feel reasonably satisfied with what you have written.

There are many different methods of priming the pump of creativity. Just as we exercise our bodies, so too we need to exercise our brains, and any writing you do as a warm-up is valuable preparation for the task of starting your novel.

Shaping an idea into a plot

You may actually have lots of story ideas but lack the confidence to believe in their creative possibilities. It's just an idea, you may say. How in the world can I tell if it's enough to turn into a full length plot?

Try to keep in mind that an idea is all that professional writers start with too. Fully developed plots do not fall from heaven. What experienced writers learn is how to test ideas to see if they have enough going for them to sustain a book length story.

This is where the hard work really starts. Ideas must be played with, worried at, filtered through the subconscious. This process doesn't happen easily and it takes time. For me, 80 per cent of the work of producing a novel is the thinking that goes on beforehand in developing the plot.

Often the idea that originally stirred my imagination will mutate or even vanish, but it will have catalyzed the evolution of another idea that is strong enough to develop into a full length novel.

An idea needs 'thickening', it needs complications and embellishment to give it momentum and depth. As your imagination plays with a particular idea that interests you, you should be striving to visualize scenes, incidents, action. But to sustain an entire plotline, action needs to have significant consequences which by the end of the story have caused the lead character to change or develop.

My starting point in the development of any idea that interests me is to ask myself: **Does this idea allow me the scope to develop a character with strong desires opposed by equally strong forces?**

In other words, does the idea offer the potential for conflict? Because **without conflict you have no story.**

Read that sentence again. And again.

Plotting for the popular fiction market is all about creating conflict and problems for your characters. The storyline evolves from how your characters are going to have to act as a result of their problems.

There is no story without conflict. Popular fiction is always about the struggle of your lead character to achieve something in the face of opposing forces.

At the same time it is vital that your heroine's particular goal be a significant one. You can hardly sustain reader interest in a heroine who simply wants to get the sports page edited by a woman so that women's sport gets a look-in!

Something important must be at stake—and this should create serious conflict for your heroine.

Say, for example, she is a lawyer determined to prove her client's innocence. As a result she comes up against some of the city's most powerful and wealthy citizens. Or she could be the whistle-blower driven to expose corruption; the woman who wants to regain her rightful inheritance; the policewoman who infiltrates a dangerous gang to break up a crime ring.

Now you may say, quite rightly, that at first glance there's not too much that's original in those ideas. But what if, in the last instance, for example, the policewoman finds her own brother is the Mister Big? All of a sudden the story is given greater depth and dimension by the addition of this interesting moral dilemma—on both sides. Does the officer overlook the ties of blood to bring her brother to justice? Can the villain bring himself to order a hit on his own sibling?

Take the case of the lawyer. What if she falls in love only to discover that her lover is the son of the man who has framed her client? Is the son in the know? Is our heroine being used? Is her life in danger?

These are the sorts of questions that help you to flesh out the skeleton of the classic plot outline and at the same time develop characters of depth.

How much of the plot do you need to know before you start?

As I said before, it is not necessary to have every detail of your plot worked out before you start writing. **I've always held the view that if you wait until you have what you think is the perfect plot you may never begin!**

Of course there are writers who like to have everything worked out beforehand. Having a detailed synopsis of the entire story makes them feel secure and happy. They know exactly where they are going, what is going to happen every step of the way. That's fine too. There are certainly no hard-and-fast rules where creativity is concerned.

But for myself, and I suspect the majority of writers, the approach is much less structured.

When an idea for a book is starting to hatch in my brain, I let my subconscious play with it without struggling too much to give it form. There are certain times of the day when the subconscious is more accessible than usual. I find the twilight zone just before falling asleep or waking up, when the mind is less busy with the prosaic problems of everyday living, a perfect time to let my thoughts wander at random. No matter how vague an idea, if it has any promise at all, I jot it down in the notebook I keep beside my bed. Another time I find useful for pondering ideas is when I'm engaged in such mechanical tasks as driving or gardening.

In my own case I find ideas are best developed in solitude and peace. It is in states bordering on self-hypnosis that plotting happens step by tiny step. I scribble down notes on personality, incident, detail and background until the initial idea has acquired substance and reality and I feel I finally know enough about my storyline and characters to begin to write. A further—and essential—yardstick is the sense of excitement bubbling inside me which tells me this is a story I *have* to write.

But even when at last I sit down at the computer to begin, I still don't have every detail of the story in my head.

And that's the way I like it. Writing is a creative process. The joy and thrill are in the surprises I give myself as the story unfolds. If I knew everything before I started I'm sure I'd be bored!

The essentials: Motivation and conflict

There are, however, two essential questions I must be able to answer before I begin. **What does this character want?** That is, what is my heroine's motivation? And **who or what is getting in the way of her achieving her goals?** This provides the conflict.

Only when I know my characters needs can I start to create obstacles to those goals.

Once I can answer the two questions above, I have the knowledge I require to make various other decisions about locale, the love interest, sub-plot(s) and so on. At this stage I make sure I can visualize a strong opening, various significant incidents in the middle, and the crisis that will lead to the ending.

By now, too, I have enough experience to know that I may end up writing a different beginning—or ending—than I first envisaged, and that this doesn't matter a bit. The important thing at this stage is to be able to visualize a succession of scenes. In other words, my idea has to have enough momentum to drive the plot.

As long as I have the conflict/motivation firmly established, it doesn't worry me that I haven't solved the little problems—like deciding how to have a character get out of jail, survive a murder attempt, gain access to secret documents. Experience has taught me that by the time I reach that part of the story other things will have occurred that will help me solve these problems.

On the other hand, earlier events in the story may have so altered in the writing that my heroine may not end up in jail at all. So I refuse to worry beforehand about something that may never happen!

All I can recommend is that you learn to trust your subconscious to solve the details of your story as they arise.

What comes first—plot or character?

This is a common question asked by beginner writers. I really don't think it's possible to work on plot in isolation from character. At the same time that I am mulling over an idea that interests me, I am also considering the sort of character who could bring that idea to life.

Or I may already have an interesting character in mind, then start searching for the motivation/conflict that will propel that character into action.

Thinking can't be compartmentalized. Ideas for the plot may direct my invention of characters or vice versa. All the elements of the story are steadily built up together. In this chapter, however, I will deal chiefly with questions of plot.

The classic plot

Here is a guide to the format of the classic plot.

At the beginning

- Open with a 'hook'—some dramatic, suspenseful, exciting incident—which sets the tone of the story. This can often mean starting with a prologue in which the main character faces a crisis before splitting off into flashback to fill in the rest of the storyline.

- Introduce the main character as soon as possible.

- State the serious problem faced by your heroine. She must want or need something very badly. Make sure it is something of consequence.

- Make clear where and when the story is set.

- Establish the villain and reveal how his or her wants are in direct opposition to those of your heroine.

- Show the emotional relationship between the heroine and the other important characters. The romantic interest can be established here.

- Establish sub-plots.

In the middle section of your story

- The heroine attempts to solve her problem. There are temporary triumphs but the problem intensifies.

- The villain is actively involved in putting obstacles in the way of the heroine's attempt to solve her problem.

- The relationships between the major characters develop.

- The sub-plots are further developed.

- Complication is piled on complication until the heroine is faced with her worst moment.

Which brings us to

The ending

- A new incident or stimulus provides a breakthrough that encourages the heroine to struggle on.

- The villain sets the last, seemingly insurmountable obstacle.

- The heroine manages to beat the odds and the villain is defeated.

- Loose ends are tied up. This is also the place for a surprise twist, if you're clever enough to come up with one!

It may surprise you to learn that when I wrote my first novel I had little or no idea of these guidelines. What I *did* know was that I really enjoyed books which started with an intriguing premise, which had a likeable, intelligent main character faced with a serious problem and an equally determined adversary, which showed that main character struggling against setback after setback, and which had me on the edge of my seat by the closing pages. When I started to write, that's the sort of story that developed: the sort of story I like to read.

If the guidelines I've given seem to you to be a formula, then all I can say is that it's a formula that works—just ask Hollywood, which produces dozens of multi-million-dollar movies a year following a similar pattern. The story of Good struggling and winning through against Evil is one that has been told over and over again down the centuries. Of course that same struggle can be couched in literary terms, but not all of us want to be, or can be, literary writers. The great mass of readers, on the other hand, buy books that promise escape and entertainment.

If your goal is to reach as wide a reading public as possible, you'd do well to note the conventions that have proved their wide appeal for so long.

What about originality?

Sometimes would-be writers are daunted by the belief that their plot must be sensational, utterly original, never written before.

Certainly there are novels that have truly original storylines, but they are rare. Yet readers still find plenty to enjoy in the masses of other novels that continue to be published.

So while your idea may have been used many times before, it is your own emotional attachment to that idea that gives it your personal stamp and can make it a hit with readers.

Originality in plotting comes from the uniqueness of your own outlook on life. And that is the product of your personal background and experiences. The theory advanced by Dorothea Brande in her famous book, *Becoming a Writer* (Jeremy P. Tarcher Inc, 1934) is that each of us, as a result of our life experiences, already carries in our own 'unconscious'—as Brande calls the part of our mind just below the threshold of conscious awareness—certain dramatic dilemmas, character types, emotional responses and backgrounds that we wish to explore.

Once our 'type' of story rises in our unconscious, our conscious mind alters and shapes it to give it the freshness needed for each new novel we write. It is in the conscious, says Brande that the idea is 'scrutinized, pruned, altered, strengthened, made more spectacular or less melodramatic'.

As a would-be writer you must learn to tap into and explore the 'unconscious', to meander through the landscape of your own mind, as it were. This usually needs solitude and quiet, with no distractions. During such a period of reverie, random ideas and images emerge that can set off whole cascades of thought.

Because I have found many of the solutions to my writing problems this way, I have great faith in my subconscious. I know its power. What is vital, however, is to always note down those ideas that seem promising. I know through hard personal experience that ideas not jotted down will almost certainly be forgotten.

Tapping emotional experience

I haven't yet mentioned the role played in plot development by first-hand experiences.

Always bear in mind that readers of popular fiction want a well-written story that takes them on a roller-coaster ride from the vicarious thrill of facing danger to the joy of falling in love, the pleasure of success, even the agony of loss.

Like actors, writers draw on experiences in their own lives to bring emotional intensity to their work. Instead of denying or trying to ignore your emotional reactions, as a writer you should strive to be open and receptive. All emotional experience offers something that can be mined and used in your work. As a writer your words will come straight from the heart when you are able to recall a similar emotional state to the one you are re-creating on the page.

In *Indecent Ambition*, Lenore, my young heroine, is present at the death of the old woman who brought her up. When I wrote the scene I was recapturing the emotions engendered by visiting my own grandmother as she lay close to death. I recalled her peaceful face—the thin, blue veins under the fine, pale skin—and as I held her bony, paper-dry hand it seemed to me that I was gripping a tentative last thread between the world of the living and whatever lay after. I drew on that memory to write the scene:

> Lenore looked down into Nan's pallid face, the skin as crumpled as old parchment.
>
> She forced her dry lips apart. 'Nan … it's me. Lenore. I'm here.' Her voice was hoarse with emotion as she took Nan's cold, thin hand in her own.
>
> Slowly, Nan lifted tired, heavy eyes to look at the young woman who stood beside her hospital bed. In a sudden flash of energy a smile touched those eyes in their nests of wrinkles.
>
> 'Lenore, my love … oh, I'm so glad you're here.' The words came out in a harsh, broken whisper and she clutched weakly at Lenore's hand.

In another part of the same book I recall the emotional experience of packing away my dead father's clothes. The photograph I describe was one given to me by my grandmother after his death.

> It was a heartbreaking task to sort through dinner jackets, sweaters, handmade shirts, to pack away her father's beloved tennis racquets, his favorite sneakers.
>
> And the tears spilled down her cheeks when she found, carefully stored away in a cupboard in his study, a framed photo of herself at the age of six. A lock of her

fine baby hair lay with it under the glass. On the mount had been written, in her father's hand, 'My love, my future, my life.'

These incidents occurred long before I became a writer but the poignancy stayed with me.

A notebook is an invaluable aid to recalling emotional states, both positive and negative. Harnessing your own emotional experience in the difficult process of spawning a plot can help give the necessary momentum and conviction to an idea. Incidents and scenes can be visualized—and written about—much more clearly when you can also feel the emotions associated with them.

Forget the ordinary, make it larger than life

Experienced writers always have their professional antennas tuned for the offbeat or unusual situation that can be made plausible. It is usually the novice who worries that an idea is too 'over-the-top' to be acceptable.

As a beginner you may feel that the story you are writing should be scrupulously true to life. But have you watched TV recently? Been to the movies? Fictional characters and events are of necessity larger than life. Readers of popular fiction want an escape from the ordinary and every day. They *want* to suspend their disbelief and be carried into a world different from their own.

Yet this doesn't mean you should underestimate the intelligence of your readers. Overblown plotlines will be accepted only if you achieve credibility by providing realistic detail and strong characterization.

As a writer you can get away with creating an incredible storyline if you make sure you draw credible characters. Readers will accept almost any fictional situation—it's only sloppy craftsmanship that will make them toss away a book in disgust.

Sub-plots are mini-plots

The main plot ideally runs through the whole story. It should be the focus of the beginning and provide the final climax.

Sub-plots are used to add depth and interest to an otherwise straight-through plotline and to help avoid a too-predictable outcome. **The trick is to weave sub-plots into the main story** so they don't appear as mere padding.

In the planning stage of your novel you should try to make as many connections between the sub-plot(s) and the main plot as possible. You can do this by having incidents in the main plot affect what is happening in the sub-plot—and vice versa—as well as having main-plot characters operate within the context of the sub-plot.

There are no rules about how many sub-plots you may or may not have. If you are going to introduce more than one, however, make sure that the main plot is up and running before you introduce the sub-plot. This ensures that the lead character and the main plot are sufficiently well established so that readers won't be confused by seeming sidetracks and interruptions to the main story.

Sub-plots need just as much thought and effort as the main plot. They, too, should be well thought-out, with beginning, middle and end as well as their share of crises and surprises.

Sometimes a sub-plot may run only a short way through the story before being resolved; at other times it may continue to run parallel to the main story until close to the end. To avoid anticlimax, sub-plots should be resolved before the main plot.

Sub-plots are also used to help bring the heroine closer to a solution of the main plot problem or to present an obstacle to the solution of the main plot. For example, a sub-plot character has some vital information. Because of some problem in her own life, which is described in the sub-plot, she needs money desperately. She therefore decides to sell her information to the heroine and in so doing helps the heroine solve her own problems. Alternatively, after getting in touch with the heroine and offering to sell the information, the minor character may be killed before their meeting. This presents an obstacle for the heroine but can also be a turning point that leads her investigations in a different direction.

This last example also demonstrates how sub-plots can be used to generate suspense. While you don't want to dispatch your heroine, killing off a minor character can underline the threat to your main character.

Another way to keep readers turning the pages is to cut from the main plot to the sub-plot at a dramatic moment. For example, say the heroine is about to enter the building where, unknown to her, the murderer is waiting. If this is going to be the climactic scene, you should now pick up the thread of your sub-plot and resolve it before returning to the big-bang scene which will lead to the resolution of the main plot.

Sometimes as a beginner writer you may have trouble differentiating between the main plot and a sub-plot as you are formulating your story. If so, ask yourself where most of the action takes place. This should always be in the main plot.

In the next chapter I will take you step by step through the process by which I shaped the plot of my first novel.

Chapter 3: Anatomy Of A Novel

How *Indecent Ambition* was plotted

I hope that by offering you an insight into how my first novel came into being I'll be able to demonstrate how an initial concept slowly develops into a full-fledged storyline.

Motivation

As I hope I've made clear, strong motivation is one of the essentials of good plotting. *Indecent Ambition* centers on a woman with political ambitions. The goal of my heroine, Anthea James, is to become Prime Minister for reasons that are rooted deeply in her past.

This idea appealed to me for two reasons, first because I am interested in politics generally and second because I was keen to attempt a woman's story from a different angle. In most of the popular fiction being published at the time, the heroines were making it in the traditional 'women's' fields of fashion, movies, marketing and so on.

Yet I knew that political ambition alone was not sufficient motivation for my heroine. Readers would find little to identify with if Anthea was only interested in the trappings of power. I had to ensure that her drive and ambition evolved very much from her background. As part of the process of giving credibility to my heroine's motivation, I decided to have her raised by Nan Reilly, an Irishwoman in her 60s, who ran Sydney's most infamous brothel.

In mulling over the problem, I decided it would be best to have Anthea start out knowing nothing about Nan's 'business'. Instead,

Nan would appear merely as her kindly landlady, taking pity on a homeless child whose father had been killed.

Yet ultimately I needed to have Anthea discover the truth about the source of Nan's wealth. Firstly to have her see at first-hand what some women had to face when denied valid options and opportunities and thus light the spark of her political ambition, and secondly, to give her a past she would need to keep hidden as she began her political ascent.

During these early ponderings I had to decide just how Anthea would find out Nan's secret. I made up my mind that Nan would fall ill and be forced to ask her young protégée to take charge of her business. This obviated the need for Anthea to work as a prostitute and allowed me to keep reader sympathy for my heroine by clearly showing her abhorrence of Nan's true profession. Finally, Anthea only reluctantly agrees to help Nan because of the debt she feels she owes her. And, of course, by putting my heroine in this situation I was able to add credibility to her motivation for political power which would enable her to achieve real changes in the opportunities for women.

It was the idea for the character that came to me first—but it instantly began to suggest the plot. Right from the start, I wanted to steer away from stereotypes. If Anthea was going to become prime minister, she could not be too young; nor did I want to paint her as a raving beauty. Certainly she would be attractive, but the assets I most wanted to stress were her intelligence, determination and astuteness.

As well, although she would be moving in a man's world, I wanted to emphasize the facts that Anthea was totally feminine, all woman—and that she would achieve her goals through her own efforts.

On both these points it is the author speaking here of course! My private view is that women can achieve success without having to become honorary men. I also believe women can only achieve equality if they are financially independent. I have already stressed the need to feel passionate about what you write. In Anthea James I had the essence of a character who would be the mouthpiece for some very strong feelings of my own.

So here were my major problems solved—I had a character I cared about, one who was strongly motivated to achieve a significant goal.

I next had to decide what Anthea would do between leaving life with Nan and eventually seeking office. This is where a beginner writer has to be careful. It would have been a mistake on my part merely to think up some fill-in career that I could cover in a chapter or so before getting back to the main story. Remember, you goal is to try to build a character that readers can come to admire and care for. At the same time, this character has to grow and develop so that by the end of the story she is changed in some significant way.

With this in mind, I didn't brush over Anthea's intervening years. Rather I used them to achieve all of these aims. I traced her evolution from a young, naive girl to an astute, sophisticated woman who made her initial mark as a media personality. And no lightweight either. I made her one of the most respected women in the Australian media, a role model for thousands who drew inspiration from her success and who admired her empathy with them and their problems.

By drawing this contrast between my character's public image and her secret background, I was able to add to the suspense created when Anthea found herself at risk of exposure.

Conflict

Once I had my lead character and had worked out her motivation, I needed to decide how to introduce conflict into the story. In other words, I had to devise a character or characters who would provide serious opposition to Anthea and her plans.

Someone as powerful as my heroine needed a pretty strong opponent. The villain I decided on was Julian Crane, Anthea's employer and a powerful media baron. Because it is important to find ways to keep major characters interacting, I placed them in the same arena—their workplace.

At first I wasn't quite sure what grounds might exist for serious conflict between my heroine and my villain. Only as I worked on other levels of the story did these slowly develop.

Meanwhile, I still needed a love interest. I decided that this would be Anthea's first love, David Yarrow. To create suspense, I also decided that he would reappear in my heroine's life at a crucial moment.

The character of David Yarrow was a deliberate attempt at snaring an American readership. I decided that while David would be Australian-born, he would have grown up in the US. When he returns to Australia he is a media mogul, which would place him, too, in a common arena with Anthea. Although I have lived for short times in the US it was not necessary to give the reader great detail about David's life there. All I had to relate about his past was what was required to provide momentum and motivation in the present. This would be supplied by a flashback to the time in his youth when he and Anthea had first met and by his disclosure of his present aim: challenging the Crane media empire. I was thus giving David something to do, not having him exist just to provide the love interest for my heroine.

The relationship between my two major characters also gave me plenty of scope to add suspense to the story. When David left Anthea with cruel suddenness years before, it was because he was convinced she was part of Nan's business. So when they meet again 20-odd years later, Anthea runs the risk of exposure if David recognizes her.

But when the story opens in the present, with Anthea just about to make her move into politics, David is not yet on the scene. I figured though, that a woman in her late 30s definitely needed a lover, so I invented Alex Volka, one of Sydney's most eligible bachelors. Again, there was nothing haphazard about my choice of a career for him. By making Alex a well-known barrister investigating the extent of organized crime in Australia, I gave him and Anthea a common purpose which keeps them appearing together in the story.

As I gradually worked through my character ideas I made notes and added them to my file. I was also chewing over a number of sub-plots and began to feel excited enough about the story to want to start writing. But I was still stumped about the major point of conflict with my villain.

As I have said, all writing is excellent practice for getting the creative juices flowing. So with the problem of the major conflict not yet worked out precisely, I sat down and began.

After I had written the first fifteen or so pages I was excited to find myself gaining an even stronger sense of my main characters as well as a feeling of satisfaction about finally having started my book. Beginning to write before I have everything perfectly pieced together usually works for me. As long as I have developed a strong enough motivation and can easily visualize my main characters, I find that in eight cases out of ten the few remaining problems can be worked out once I actually begin to write.

On the other hand, if the motivation *isn't* well enough developed this becomes obvious within the first few pages. At that stage I can try to pinpoint the weaknesses I must then work through before continuing or, alternatively, I am able to see that even if the motivation problem can be overcome the storyline itself doesn't excite me enough to make me want to go on.

Sub-plot

I was still mulling over possibilities for the conflict and for various sub-plots when a newspaper story caught my eye. It was exactly what I was looking for! Now I could base the conflict between my heroine and the villain on fact.

The newspaper article gave details about young Asian women who were being lured to Australia with the promise of well-paid jobs and then finding themselves forced to work in brothels.

This real-life detail gave me the perfect material to flesh out my story and keep my heroine *active*. Instead of just writing about Anthea's political campaign, which mightn't have been very exciting in itself, I could now show her in her media role investigating rumors of what was a true story.

At the same time, the reference to brothels would also tie in neatly to Anthea's background with Nan and, even more vitally, would finally allow me to develop a point of real conflict with Julian Crane. To avoid spoiling the story for those who haven't read it, I'm not going to elaborate on that angle!

You will recall my emphasis on conflict and complications in previous chapters. These elements are why another sub-plot in *Indecent Ambition* involves a young American heiress. Kelly Delamar not only adds further conflict and complications to the political campaign/brothel investigation scenario which is part of the main plot, but also becomes an obstacle in the relationship between Anthea and David. I achieved the latter goal by making Kelly obsessed with David and determined to marry him.

Other sub-plots evolved as I saw the need to develop other aspects of the storyline. These include the relationship between Julian Crane's wife and a toy boy lover, and a young reporter's love for Kelly. As they should be, all the sub-plots are developed from and closely interwoven with the main storyline. They were never padding. All were vital to the structure of the story.

Locale and background

In *Indecent Ambition* locale and background were chosen deliberately. First, I realized that no other writer had yet used an Australian background for a mass market novel of this type. At the same time, the plot had to be developed so I could place my heroine in various foreign settings to extend my readership. The backgrounds I used—Sydney, London, LA, Paris, Rome—would appeal, I knew, to most readers of popular fiction. The research was minimal as I had lived, or spent some time, in each of these places. Detail on unfamiliar local backgrounds was easily obtained—

although readers still like to point out that there are no white-sand beaches in Cairns. Which only highlights the advantage of paying a personal visit to your chosen locales!

The ending

At the start I had only a vague idea of the ending—that my heroine would end up in serious jeopardy. It didn't turn out quite the way I imagined, but by the time I reached that point in the writing I had no problem achieving a dramatic and satisfying finish. Finally the loose ends were drawn together in a very short epilogue.

Call it the luck of the ignorant, but in writing *Indecent Ambition* I never faced a serious moment of writer's block or doubt about where my story was going. I am sure doing all the research on successful fiction helped, but also perhaps, the fact that this was a first novel meant I had nothing to lose but my time. The other advantages in writing a first novel are the lack of pressure or expectations and the huge pool of fresh ideas to choose from. The success of *Indecent Ambition* however, made the writing of my second novel one of the hardest tasks I ever set myself.

But that's another story!

Exercise 1

Pick a popular novel you have read and enjoyed.

Identify the main character.

What is the main problem or conflict faced by that character?

In no more than three or four sentences, give an outline of the plot.

Identify the antagonist(s). What is his/her goal?

Identify the sub-plot(s), if any.

Identify the romantic interest.

Is the time span important in this story?

What is the physical setting?

How is the conflict/problem solved?

Is there a twist at the end?

Chapter 4: Who's The Guy With The Pimple On His Nose?

Creating characters

In popular fiction, readers expect a lead character they can identify with and barrack for.

Because the main character must carry the plot, credible characterization is essential. A character who is drawn well enhances the plausibility of your story line. By making characters believable, you gain greater acceptance for the extreme plot devices and larger-than-life scenarios that are often a feature of popular fiction.

My books all evolved from an interest in developing a particular character through whom I could explore various issues of interest to me. The lead characters in my novels are female, but I also find little trouble in getting into the skin of my male characters. Perhaps this is because I have always had relaxed and easy relationships with men and enjoy learning what makes them tick. Writing from the male point of view is something I find interesting and challenging.

However, having said all that, I rarely sit down and work out a very detailed biography of each major character before I start.

Of much greater interest to me are the personality and psychological profiles I devise for them, my heroine in particular. And what matters most are those aspects of the profiles which are going to make my story happen.

To my way of thinking it is no use wasting time developing interesting personality traits for a character if those traits are of no pertinence to the story.

In popular fiction there is no room for rambling or unnecessary detail. Everything must be focused on developing the plot. So even if you are fascinated by the fact that your lead character was a poor student who didn't learn to read until she was ten, this point can only be a distraction if it does not help to drive the story forward.

Where do you get ideas for characters?

The same place you get ideas for plots: from reading, observing, and from your own imagination. Characters may be suggested by real people, drawn from aspects of ourselves, or whipped out of thin air.

However, I don't think it's a good idea to base your characters too closely on real people. Not only is there the risk of libel, but using a real person can actually be a handicap. Whatever image you already have of a person can hinder your attempts to develop him or her into the sort of character required to tell your story. Those preconceived ideas make it difficult to put your own stamp on the character you are trying to create. To make a character your own means developing a personality and temperament for her that are going to work within the context of the story you intend telling.

This is not to say that, as with plot ideas, you shouldn't use triggers from real life to stir your imagination. But from that point on, the character has to become your own creation, the vehicle you need to tell your own particular story.

Main characters

One of the first tasks when you begin your novel is to make sure the reader knows whose story is being told. This means introducing the main character as soon as possible. Having said this, I am forced to reveal that not all of my own novels begins with the heroine on page one. But I make very sure she's there and leading the show within at least the next couple of pages.

What makes a character believable?

1. Strong and plausible motivation.

2. Appropriate psychological profile.

3. Change and development.

Motivation we have already defined as whatever drives your heroine to act. Her psychological profile helps bring your heroine to life. By offering your readers an understanding of your heroine's inner life, you help them understand her motives for behaving as she does.

In other words, **motivation is *what* drives your heroine to act, while her psychological profile reveals *why* she acts the way she does.**

A main character also gains credibility and leaves readers satisfied when, by the end of the story, she is changed in some significant way.

By the end of *Indecent Ambition* a confused, naive young girl fearful of love has developed into a strong, fulfilled woman. By the end of my second novel, *Whisper Her Name*, (print published as '*Angel of Honor*') a spoilt, willful adolescent has become a mature, resourceful and dynamic leader.

Creating heroes and heroines that readers can identify with

Heroes and heroines in books, movies and real life exhibit many of the qualities we all admire. Aren't we all impressed by people who are brave, competent, kind, generous, intelligent and resourceful? Remember that if readers don't like your lead character they won't care a hoot what happens to her. There are a few notable exceptions to this rule, for example, Scarlett O'Hara in *Gone With The Wind*. Scarlett was spoilt and headstrong and her actions were not always squeaky clean, but whether readers loved or hated her she elicited a strong emotional response and in the balance her good points outweighed her bad. In the same way, there have been quite a few male lead characters in crime/police novels who have various quirks or personality defects but essentially they are motivated by doing the right thing.

So in other words, it shouldn't be necessary for your heroine to cheat, lie or defraud or incriminate others as she sets about solving her problem. Yet this isn't to say she has to be a saint who can't lose her temper occasionally, break the speed limit, or tell the odd white lie when necessary. It might be best though to avoid the sort of desperate situation in which your heroine is forced to kill to save herself or someone she loves.

Sometimes, however, you may find that such an extreme response is the only way out of her dilemma. If this is the case, and even when the villain deserves what he or she gets, it is vital that you show your heroine being deeply affected by her actions. No reader to going to have much sympathy for a heroine who kills and then goes out to dinner!

A dilemma like this occurred in *Indecent Ambition,* when in the climactic physical fight one of the sympathetic characters was forced to save another character's life by killing the villain.

The villain deserved his end, but it was still vital that I clearly show my character's trauma over what she was forced to do. I should also point out that the character in question was not the main character. What is more, I used her suffering over the incident to bring about a closer bond with the heroine. Most importantly, however, I was able to justify her action to the readers.

Another way to destroy readers' admiration for your heroine is to have her act like a mindless fool. You may think that by making her forget her passport so she can't follow the villain over the border you're adding suspense to your story, but all you are really doing is making your heroine look stupid. To sustain reader identification, your main character should act with resourcefulness and intelligence, and be brave, capable and competent.

I hope I'm not making you think you have to create some paragon of virtue, a stereotype of perfection. That's certainly not the case, because readers will probably have every bit as much trouble identifying with a saint as with a sinner. No, what I am suggesting is that minor flaws and blemishes help to add depth and interest to your characters. Maybe she's quick-tempered, impulsive or shy. Perhaps she lets her career interfere with her personal relationships. It's these sorts of imperfections that add credibility to your lead character.

Credible villains

It's just as important for your bad guys—I refer to them here as male though of course they can just as easily be female—to be more than mere cardboard cut outs. Make your antagonist a worthy opponent for your heroine and both of them will gain greater depth and credibility.

For your villain, motivation is every bit as essential as it is for your heroine. Your bad guy must be driven to reach his goal as powerfully as your heroine is to reach hers—and of course these goals are always opposed.

With their ruthlessness and various quirks, villains can actually be much more interesting to create than main characters. Imagine, for example, a killer who is also a wonderful father, husband or son. Or a ruthless business rival who was once a priest.

Take the time to develop an interesting psychological profile for your villain and you will have a better backdrop against which to bring your heroine—and of course the storyline—to life.

Avoiding stereotypes

Sometimes you can become so involved in thinking out the twists of the plot that you take the easy way out with characters. But you have to do the hard work here too. Readers don't want another story with the predictable whore with the heart of gold, the drunken Irishman, the shy virgin. One-dimensional characters are boring and lack credibility. And characters who don't develop through the story, who aren't changed as a result of their experiences, also fail to convince. It is important to let readers see the growth of your character by showing her reaction to the chain of events that make up your storyline.

Starting from scratch

Let's do a little exercise in creating a character. It should prove to you how inextricably plot and character are linked.

Let's say you decide on a heroine who is going to bust a scam involving crooked business deals. Her motivation might be that her brother, let's call him Rob, was a former employee of the company concerned and was made to take the rap for one of the illegal deals. Expanding on the idea, we could have Rob either killed or committing suicide in jail. Kate, our heroine, believed her brother when he swore he was innocent of the charges. Therefore his death gives Kate a strong motivation to bring the villains to justice … I'm beginning to warm to this idea already!

Okay, let's see how we add flesh to both the basic plot idea and the character of Kate. To begin with, we do have a strong motivation for our heroine. She is seeking to uncover the scam that led to her brother's death. Obviously if they fought like cat and dog, if she despised everything about him, she wouldn't have much incentive to clear his name. So we can assume they must have been close. This assumption immediately indicates what details of Kate's background it will be necessary to fill in.

Imagine her childhood: Was elder brother Rob someone she always looked up to? Why? Did he help to bring her up when their parents were killed? Was Kate born with a medical disorder and did Rob take a second job to help with the hospital bills? Start thinking along these lines and I'm sure you will come up with a background that strengthens Kate's motivation to discover the truth about her brother's death and to bring the villains to justice.

These goals also enable you to show your heroine's heroic qualities: her love for and loyalty to her brother, her determination and resourcefulness to expose the villains and clear his name, her intelligence and courage.

The next step is to decide how to get Kate *actively* involved with the villains. One starting point may be to make her a bright MBA and have her apply for a job in the crooked company. It goes without saying that she would do everything possible to conceal her relationship to Rob.

The MBA idea is okay, but why not look at things in a more imaginative way? What if Kate were a dentist or in advertising, and therefore lacked the necessary formal business qualifications? This makes her task a little harder but enables us to reveal her resourcefulness in finding a way into the company's stronghold.

One option could be to have her take a job as a waitress in the canteen. Now she has access to the building and a cover that may enable her to pick up information that will help expose the crooks.

At this point let's not forget that popular fiction readers expect a love interest for the main character. Best-selling authors from Jeffrey Archer to John Grisham know the importance of incorporating a romantic angle in their plots. It was for this reason that I decided to make Kate's brother the victim. This leaves the way open to developing a love interest for Kate. If, instead, I had her actions motivated by the loss of a lover, it would be stretching credibility to show our heroine obsessed with justice for one man while falling in love with another!

Bringing the character to life

To me, it's much more important to have worked through my heroine's motivation and psychological profile before I give two seconds' thought to her appearance.

This is partly because the heroine's background details will often determine her physical ones.

For example, Kate can't be too young if she already has an MBA, as she would have spent years studying and gaining experience. It is factors like these which help to define our characters' physical appearance.

However you decide to describe your main character, make sure you keep the detail relevant. For example, if we're going to make a huge fuss about Kate's long red hair, we should only do so if we are going to make use of the fact later in the story. This could happen if, say, Kate disappears. When her distraught lover goes looking for her it would be well within the bounds of credibility to have someone remember the girl with the long red hair.

The point is that if the hair colour isn't going to be pertinent to the storyline, don't make a big thing of it.

What Kate wears also tells us about her personality. Does she appear very straitlaced at the office but more feminine at home? Do clothes matter to her? Does she spend freely on jewelry? Or does she own just a few good pieces she inherited from that poor dead mother? The point in considering all these questions is to paint in only the details required to give us a picture of our heroine. Pages and pages of description are not necessary. To most readers of popular fiction, over-long passages of description only hinder the pace of the story.

Where description is necessary, the rule is: *show*, don't *tell*.

Telling:

Kate was a tall, attractive blonde.

Showing:

Kate had inherited her father's height and her mother's fine English skin. Even with her pale long hair drawn severely back she had the sort of looks that made men turn their heads.

It's not necessary to paint the whole picture at once. A couple of paragraphs later we could mention our heroine's eye colour, perhaps, and at the same time, something about her character:

> She looked at him with those intelligent, assessing grey eyes. 'You're lying to me, aren't you?'

Now we know not only the colour of Kate's eyes but something about her understanding of human nature—and her ability to exploit it.

When you want to fix a character's appearance in your reader's mind, the rule of three can help. This means focusing on three physical characteristics and repeating them within a couple of pages. In the above example we get a quick mental picture of Kate from the description of her hair, eyes, height and skin. The idea is to refer to these same points again soon afterward.

> Kate listened in silence, her grey eyes never leaving his face.

> **Or**: She pushed back a strand of fine, fair hair.

> **Or**: At around six feet, Jock Lawson was just an inch or two taller than Kate herself.

In this last example I've illustrated how to kill two birds with one stone—reiterating Kate's height while at the same time describing another character.

I strongly suggest that every time you introduce new characters you note down their age and the colour of their eyes and hair. That way you won't have to flip back and forth through your typed pages trying to ascertain whether Maureen is a blonde or a brunette!

Another way characters can be defined is by the way they speak. In the chapter on dialogue I will show how speech can be used to indicate background, age and education.

Characters can also be brought to life by describing their mannerisms or interests. Maybe your heroine drives too fast or is obsessively tidy. Perhaps she hates cooking, enjoys classical music, and is a pet lover. Again, there's no need to make a fuss of such details, but when they are woven into a story, they help to flesh out your characters:

> *The stop-start traffic drove Kate to distraction. Impatiently she drummed her fingers on the leather-bound steering wheel. It was the same impatience she displayed in her career: anything that impeded her progress was a major irritation.*

This gives insight into our heroine's character. The reader learns much more than if we had merely written: 'Kate was an impatient driver.'

Once you understand the psychological core of your character you can find ways to express it. Is your heroine an introvert? Extrovert? Sophisticated? Naive? Generous? Stingy? Cautious? Aloof? Shy? Confident?

Remember, you should develop these points only as far as you need to in order to move the plot along.

In the same way, a character's skills and abilities must be referred to if they are going to be important later.

Let's say, for example, that you know your hero is going to be shipwrecked halfway through the story. This means he will need superior carpentry skills so he can patch up the yacht and sail on. But you don't wait until you reach that particular part of the story to reveal his skill with a hammer. Some casual reference should be made to it much earlier on.

This can be done as simply as by having another character pay your hero a visit and find him in his workshop. Or perhaps you could make a passing reference to a beautiful piece of furniture the hero has made for his wife's birthday. In this way you quietly lay the groundwork for what comes later.

Another way to define characters is by their physical surroundings. A completely different world is evoked by a well-kept home with grand piano and antiques than by a shared cramped apartment.

In *Indecent Ambition* I introduce my heroine, Anthea James, in the first few pages, showing her first at her place of work—the television studio—and then at home:

> The house, hidden behind a high clipped hedge overhung with muted green English trees, was Anthea's dream come true. Two storeys high, it was one of Sydney's original sandstone homes with a charm typical of its Georgian design …

> As she opened the heavy oak front door and entered the coolness of the black-and-white tiled foyer, Anthea smelt the lemon fragrance of furniture polish and saw the gleam on the French marquetry table further down the hallway. She felt a sense of satisfaction. Everything was in order, exactly as she liked it.

The house is obviously the home of a wealthy, successful stylish woman who loves order. At the same time, by saying the house is 'Anthea's dream come true', I convey that my heroine has not grown up in such splendor and thereby point to the fact that she is a self-made woman.

Later, when I describe the shabby inner-city terrace house where she grew up, the use of background re-emphasizes how far my heroine has come.

Try to remember that once characters are established they need to be consistent in manner and speech. For example, having shown Anthea as a successful, very capable career woman, I would hardly write a scene in which she has difficulty holding her own in a business meeting or is intimidated by a waiter.

Minor characters

When I begin my novels I usually know all the major characters I am going to need. But it is only as the story progresses that I develop my full cast of minor characters.

Sometimes beginner writers are unsure how much detail is required to flesh out the lesser players. Again, that depends on how large their roles are going to be. Let's go back to Kate, who is working undercover as a waitress. Obviously she would have fellow workers, but most of these don't need to be named if their roles are incidental. Or they can be portrayed as fleetingly as this:

> *Elaine, the other waitress, was nominated to show Kate the ropes. She was a thirtyish mother of two, top-heavy, with spiky dark hair and a ringing voice.*

Here's another example from *Indecent Ambition*. Anthea has arrived in Cooktown to film a segment for a report on the Bicentenary. She has a room booked at a typical country motel.

> A plump, rosy-cheeked girl wearing a shapeless blue-and-white checked dress that showed large damp patches under each over-fleshed arm came through from the back room.
>
> She greeted Anthea effusively. 'G'day. You must be the lady from the big smoke. How was the trip up? You must be pretty buggered. We're a bloody long way from Sydney, aren't we? Come on, I'll show you your room. Best in the house …'
>
> Barely stopping for breath, she hooked a key off the rack, came round from behind the counter and picked up Anthea's suitcase with seemingly little effort. She kept up the machine-gun commentary as she led a bemused Anthea up the broad flight of wooden stairs and down a chocolate-brown corridor to a room at the end.

This girl never appears in the story again. The reader doesn't need to know her name, if she's married or not, if she has brothers or sisters, or if she's a member of the local church. A string of unnecessary details will only distract from or clutter the storyline. All that's necessary is to make the character vivid enough to fulfil the role she has to play. In this last example, that meant setting the tone of the place where my heroine was to stay.

When you are introducing characters at the beginning of your story it is best not to refer to too many too quickly. We've all read the sorts of books where that occurs and know how difficult it is to keep track of who's who.

The way to overcome this problem is by introducing characters gradually and establishing each one properly before bringing in the next.

How do you do this? Again, keep in mind the rule of three. Focus on three features of the character and repeat them a couple of times to fix the picture of that person in the reader's mind.

If you reread the quick sketch of Elaine, the waitress, you'll see how I have done this with a minor character. In one short sentence I've described her in five ways—'thirtyish', 'mother of two', 'top-heavy', 'spiky dark hair', 'ringing voice'. It is the last three characteristics that *show* us Elaine. A reader wouldn't have gained any mental picture if I had merely described Elaine as a thirtyish mother of two. Again, this is an example of the difference between showing and telling.

If, however, you want Elaine to reappear later, it is important to ensure she is remembered. So when she is next referred to, pick up on some element of that earlier description that will help recall her to the reader's mind. For example:

> *'Kate!' Elaine's voice carried forcefully across the dining area, making Kate jump.*

Or:

Elaine put down the tray, overcome by a hacking cough. 'Fags,' she explained in answer to Kate's worried look. 'The kids are always naggin' me to give 'em up.'

In this way the reader is reminded that Elaine has children, while her way of speaking also helps establish her character.

Something else to watch out for in creating characters is having too many who are too similar. Characters need to be made different enough so that they stand out from each other. This means being on the lookout for too many leggy young blondes, ruthless executives, or trendy hipsters. This difference should apply to their psychological profiles as well. You wouldn't want to have three trendy bachelors all of whom hate their jobs or are bitter towards women.

Your task as a writer is to try to make your characters distinctive and memorable, not merely a blur of similar types.

Names

Choosing a name is probably more important than you realize. A lot of thought is necessary to get the right combination of names for characters.

Heroes and heroines need pleasant names that fit their personalities. Mark Kinnane gives a better impression for a hero than Joe Pittman or Arnold Bent, wouldn't you agree?

Another thing to keep in mind is that a first name capable of abbreviation should still sit well with the chosen surname. Otherwise Gerald Perry will end up as Gerry Perry!

It's just a personal thing but I also try to avoid names ending in 's'. When it comes to the possessive case things can get a little awkward. For example: Marcus's kiss ... In my own first book I could have avoided the problem of Anthea James's car, Anthea

James's show … Why didn't I just call her Anthea Sinclair?! I know I could have just used James' but that felt stilted to me too so better to avoid the problem all together.

It should be obvious, too, that names need to be chosen to suit the age and class of your characters. A 60-year-old woman would more likely be a Sharon or Tracey while her upper-middle-class counterpart might be an Olivia or Charlotte. Baby-name lists are a good place to start when you're trying to find names that fit your characters.

Something else to avoid in naming characters is having too many names starting with the same letter. It can be confusing, especially at the start of the story, to be introduced to Louise, Lyndall, Leah and Lewis. You'd be surprised how often this oversight occurs even with experienced writers.

Unusual names should be employed with care. American writers in particular seem to fancy characters called Fern or Sybellina. It's an individual choice, of course, but such unusual names give the appearance of being artificial and contrived. And too many in the one story are overkill.

Sometimes a story calls for ethnic characters. In this case it's a good idea to choose a name which is easily pronounceable (albeit mentally) by English-speaking readers. Klaus Bergmann is a better choice than Günther Schönenberger, for example.

Just remember if you make up a foreign name be sure to check it out in translation just in case the one you've chosen means Widebottom!

In my novel *Whisper Her Name*, the heroine was called Noella de Bartez. Easy enough. However, I remember that when I was trying out different surnames my subconscious came up with Valdez. That seemed fine—until I remembered it was the name of a ship which had spilled oil along the Alaskan coastline. A name with unpleasant connotations is obviously best avoided.

Whether you want to give names to very minor characters is, again, an individual choice. Some authors advise that a character who only appears once in a story should not be named. But I think there are occasions when naming and breathing a little life into a one-off character can add something to your story.

Let's take, for example, a scene in which our heroine, Kate the career woman, is in a meeting. It is interrupted by one of the company's numerous secretaries—a woman who has never been referred to before, nor will be again:

> 'I'm sorry,' Anne Clark announced, 'I'm looking for Miss Kate Grey.'

In this case, a name is distracting. Also, by naming the secretary you give the reader the impression that she's going to carry some weight in the story. In this case, therefore, where the reference is only in passing, there is no need to name the girl. All you need write is:

> 'I'm sorry,' the secretary announced...

However, where a minor character's role is small but important to the storyline, it does add life to name her or him, just as it does to provide a few background details.

In *Never Forget Me* my heroine, as a teenager, runs away from a foster home and is picked up by a long-haul truck driver. Let's see how I made the scene more vivid by giving the driver a name and a background:

> Sam Howard was dreaming.
>
> He was dreaming of the house he'd buy in Palm Springs when he won the lottery, of how he'd give Rita and the kids the life they deserved. Maids, gardeners, a swimming pool. And a tennis court for Jody who, they said, showed promise but who'd be lucky if her pa could find the dough to pay for the next season's lessons ...
>
> 'Jesus H Christ!' Swearing under his breath, Sam Howard slammed on the brakes and brought the huge semi to a grinding halt. His reverie forgotten, he wound

down the cabin window and called to the figure in the darkness. 'Hey! You all right out there?'

Try reading that passage using 'truck driver' instead of 'Sam Howard'. You'll see what I mean about ascribing names—plus a few background details—to bring minor characters to life.

Building background: A checklist

Keep an eye out for material. It's all around you, and especially now with the internet at every writers' fingertips. If I needed to fill in the background of an elderly American political character, I'd check out websites, books and articles on people like George Bush and Gerald Ford, noting their education, army careers, clubs they might have belonged to, the various jobs they held as they climbed the ladder.

Reading biographies and autobiographies is a great way to acquire background material. Make a note of everything you think you might be able to use.

One of the most difficult areas to get detailed information about can be other's people's jobs. An internet search should give you some of the details you need but I always talk to people and ask lots of questions to get more information. Some writers also find psychology texts and astrology books of value in developing a personality for their various characters. Having decided that their character is a Leo, for example, they have a ready-made psychological profile at their fingertips—determined, a leader, self-confident, outgoing. Well, at least according to the stars!

Here are some points to think about when filling in a character's background:

- Date/place of birth

- Relationship with parents/siblings

- Parents' occupation

- Childhood traumas

- Education

- Most important influence/person in childhood

- Career history

- Marital status

- Sexuality: virgin, experienced, promiscuous, enjoys sex, inhibited, good lover, guilty, fearful

- Attitude to the opposite sex

- Dreams and goals

- Ideas, values

- Successes, failures, regrets, fears

- Politics

- Attitudes to life, death, money

All this may be more than you need for your story, but it can start you thinking about what makes your particular character tick.

Chapter 5: It Was A Dark And Stormy Night

Irresistible beginnings

I can't stress strongly enough the importance of how your story begins. When a reader is facing endless offerings of books either digitally or in a bookshop, her decision to buy depends almost entirely on some or all of the following: her response to the cover, the title, the blurb—the short précis of the story—the author's name, whether she has read and enjoyed previous works by the same writer, and the opening few sentences. This is particularly true now that readers can try a 'sample' of an e-book prior to buying.

A chilling thought, isn't it? A few lines—or, if you're very lucky, one page—is all you have to grab a reader's attention and make her want to buy your book over all the others. If that fact doesn't make you direct your efforts at getting the opening right, nothing will!

In those vital beginning pages your goal must be to intrigue and entertain, to draw your reader into the action of the story as quickly as possible.

What sometimes happens however, is that you become so intent on writing an opening which never seems quite perfect that you become frustrated and disheartened. If you can't even write the opening couple of paragraphs and get them right, you ask yourself, how did you ever imagine you could complete a whole novel?

Relax. Although the opening chapter is vital, it doesn't have to be the first thing you write. If you wait until you get the perfect start you may never get any further. Always remember that the beginning can be written, or rewritten, later. I take great care over beginnings and I write and polish them again and again. But initially I might just have a 'working opening'—that is, something to get the story started but which could end up altered, embellished, or even completely different once I get the real feel of my story.

It can often be much easier to find the words to open your story when you are a few chapters into the body of it. In other cases you may spend days straining for the perfect beginning and then, as the story progresses, a different opening may come to seem more effective.

Most novelists would agree that the first 20 to 40 pages of a book are the toughest to write. It is in those opening pages that so much needs to be achieved without losing the interest of the reader. This includes introducing the main character, stating the conflict or problem she is facing, and establishing location and time. Providing the information needed to set the story in motion is called exposition.

Modern readers respond best to stories that start with both action and dialogue. It's also a good idea to indicate as soon as possible the type of story you are writing. For example, in a mystery or adventure story there should be hints of the intrigue and danger to come.

Another thing to make clear in these opening pages is through whose eyes the story is being told. The technical term for this is viewpoint. If, for example, in the first three chapters you told your story through the viewpoint of Maggie, it would be confusing to switch in Chapter 4 to Richard's viewpoint. This problem is overcome by introducing Richard as a viewpoint character much earlier so the reader is alerted to the fact that this story is being told through multiple viewpoints.

If you are having trouble deciding where exactly to begin, it's a good idea to pick a dramatic moment in your heroine's life, either at some peak of the action or at a major turning point. You might start like this:

She knew she'd have to face them sooner or later. For 48 hours now the reporters and television crews had been camped outside her home—as eager for her humiliation and defeat as they had once been to anoint her.

Angela steeled herself to open the door, feeling her stomach tighten with bitterness—and fear. Whatever happened now, it was only David who mattered.

This throws the reader right into the story and immediately raises questions. Why are the media there? What has Angela done? What is her relationship to David? And straight away we find out that this story is told from Angela's viewpoint.

What to avoid

Starting with long paragraphs of description is usually a major turn-off for the modern fiction reader. You should aim to keep the opening paragraphs short. This allows lots of 'white space' on the page. White space, or 'windows' attract readers at the start of the story, unlike daunting blocks of dense print.

As I mentioned earlier, be wary of introducing too many characters or names too quickly. If not handled deftly, this can sometimes be confusing for readers.

Another common mistake made by beginner writers is to assume that the reader has a knowledge of the essential facts. Because these facts are already familiar to you, you forget the reader doesn't know about them. For example, you may have started with a scene in which a man and woman are quarrelling. *You* know they are brother and sister, but unless you make this clear right from the start, your reader could assume they are husband and wife.

I said earlier that it's a good idea to pick up the story at a moment of dramatic action. Let's say, for example, that you decide to start with a ship in a violent storm. You write two or three graphic pages describing your character trying to survive as the vessel breaks up around her. The problem you are faced with here is that readers haven't yet established an emotional bond with the heroine, so at this stage they really couldn't care less what is happening to her. Life-and-death scenes usually work best later in the story when the reader knows the character, understands and sympathizes with her, and is fearful for her survival.

Sometimes a flash forward can be used to get your story under way. This means you begin at a dramatic point so that your reader is hooked quickly, then go back to a much earlier point in the story and advance from there until you link up once more with the opening scene.

An example of that technique is used in the opening to Angela's story above. A flash forward grabs the reader's attention. From that point we go back in time and then tell the story in proper chronological sequence until we return to the opening scene. From there the story continues to the end.

Sample starts

Because I think the way you begin your story is so vital, I am going to show you how I started two of my own novels.

From *Whisper her Name*:

> The killer was in no hurry. He knew his victim's schedule and the Citroën was parked just minutes away. He had plenty of time.

Let's examine this opening and see how much information is delivered and how many questions are raised in just a few lines to intrigue the reader and draw her quickly into the story.

I think the first sentence works to grab attention. I introduce a character who is identified not by name but by his profession—and a violent and illegal one at that. This immediately suggests an atmosphere of menace.

It is obvious also that the killer is not going to be my main character, so it might be assumed that the intended victim is the heroine. This immediately raises the questions: Who is the heroine? Why is it necessary to kill her? Who is the killer? At once the reader knows this is a novel of suspense and mystery.

Further information is given by the reference to a Citroën which suggests that the story is probably set in Europe and that is confirmed in the next couple of paragraphs.

Here is the start of *Never Forget Me:*

> He called it the Shrine.
>
> It was his secret place. His place of worship. A sanctum where the dream lived on and his fantasies could still come true.
>
> Face flushed with anticipation, the Idolator allowed his eyes to travel slowly over the walls. Her photograph was everywhere, covering every inch of space. He knew that with a flick of a switch he could hear her voice, the voice that never failed to thrill him.

As in the previous example, no name is given to the character, but look at all the questions raised that force the reader to read on!

Where is the shrine? Why is it a 'secret' place? Who is this weirdo the Idolator? Who or what is the focus of his worship? What is the dream? What are his fantasies?

You will have noticed that in neither example is the main character introduced in the opening paragraph. Instead, the aura of menace is firmly established and it is hinted that the heroine is the one at risk. Both examples are flash forwards, and the heroine is introduced within the next couple of pages.

Exposition and how to handle it

The basic purpose of exposition is to impart the information the reader needs to know to understand and believe in the characters and story. It is impossible to write a novel without using exposition.

As I hope I have already made clear, there is a big difference between showing and telling, so exposition always works best combined with description, dialogue, action and so on. Exposition should be part of the narrative flow. At the same time, you should always be trying to involve the reader on an emotional level.

Exposition is not easy. Just knowing that most writers find it difficult should help you to face and overcome this hurdle.

Most exposition occurs at the beginning of your story when you are describing characters and locale, establishing the dilemma faced by your heroine, and otherwise filling in the gaps for your readers.

Because it is essential in popular fiction to get the plot up and running first, the best way to handle exposition is to weave it as naturally as possible into the action. Keep in mind that readers are only interested in explanations after their curiosity has been aroused by something that *needs* explaining.

The way to present necessary facts is by gradually easing them into a scene. For instance, if your heroine has just inherited her father's company you might describe her arriving outside company headquarters in a limousine and entering the building. This gives you an opportunity to explore her feelings about her new position by describing the way she greets the staff and the other board members.

In this next example the exposition is handled the wrong way—by telling:

> *Anna could hardly believe it. She was now the owner of Hudson Enterprises, the company her father had built from nothing over three decades. As she made her way*

into the company foyer she couldn't help feeling nervous about her new position at the head of the international media empire.

This is showing:

Sick with nerves, Anna slid out of the limousine into Sydney's chill winter sunshine. For a moment she hesitated, her gaze slowly moving upwards to take in the skyscraper that was the heart of Hudson Enterprises. Even now, a month after her father's death, she could barely believe he was gone and that the company now belonged to her.

'Good luck, Miss Anna.' As he closed the door behind her, her chauffeur whispered his encouragement.

'Thanks, Mick.' Anna managed a smile to the man who had worked for her father for almost as long as she could remember. It was Mick Doyle who'd driven her to school on her first day, when her father had been too busy. But then Jack Hudson had always been too busy—building the media empire that crisscrossed the globe, the empire which now belonged to the 28-year-old daughter he had never really known.

Fighting back emotion, Anna climbed the steps to the glass and marble foyer.

The way to handle exposition is to make every scene serve more than one purpose. In the short piece above, we learn not only that Anna Hudson had inherited her father's media empire but also about her relationship with him, how long he's been dead, her age, the setting, her emotional state.

The idea is to introduce and develop a character, move the plot along, and establish the immediately needed background as quickly and succinctly as possible.

Another excellent technique is to let the character do the explaining by allowing the reader into her thoughts. This is shown above, where I use the chauffeur's remark to lead into Anna's inner voice, which reveals her relationship with her dead father. The use of an inner voice or thoughts is an excellent way to help readers get to know your characters—especially where there is a discrepancy between how they act or how others see them and the way they really are.

Reading successful authors can help a beginner writer learn the right techniques, but because the professionals can make it look so easy it may be useful if I also point out the wrong approach.

Here, we have Anna and a friend at lunch revealing the necessary facts rather laboriously through their conversation:

> Anna faced Lucy across the table, barely aware of the murmur of the other diners. Her voice shook with emotion.
>
> 'As you know, Lucy, since Dad died in a skiing accident I've had to take control of the company. I'm finding it really difficult.'

This is very awkward telling.

Now here's an example of less heavy-handed exposition, taken from *Indecent Ambition*. After using action and dialogue to show Anthea James at work in the television studio, I weave into the scene what readers need to know:

> At thirty-nine, Anthea James was a major success story. To her large and devoted female audience she had it all: looks, fame, wealth, success. In the eyes of her adoring fans Anthea could do no wrong. She was the woman they most admired, respected, dreamt of being.
>
> Now, as the audience of excited, chattering women began to file out of the darkened studio, Anthea stood up. As always, she knew better than to waste an

opportunity where her public image was concerned. With no appearance of haste she smoothly divested herself of her guests, promising to rejoin them soon in the network's VIP room.

As she picked her way across the cable-littered studio floor she stopped and chatted with the departing audience, those ordinary women whose lives contrasted so drably with her own. It cost her nothing and in the end could be so worthwhile.

The effect of Anthea's presence on her admirers was electrifying. That a woman as important, as successful, as frantically busy as Anthea James could spare a moment to listen, to laugh, to sympathize, made them glow with pleasure and self-importance.

Their eager eyes fed hungrily on the image she presented—the gleaming red-gold hair, the expensive understated clothes and jewelry, the full, perfect figure. To the women who clustered round her Anthea James exuded the confidence and ease of a women who has never known rejection.

Yet there was no resentment of their idol's glamour and good fortune. For, in some mysterious way, Anthea James was able to make them feel that she understood, that she knew what it might feel like to live in one of Sydney's dreary satellite suburbs with too many children and not enough money.

What they felt for her was love. Love for her compassion and concern, for her understanding of their problems and for the escape she offered from their humdrum lives. Through her weekly newspaper column, her radio phone-in program and her television show, Anthea reached out to each and every one of them. She gave them Hope.

In this passage, the reader learns about Anthea in two ways. Through her own eyes: 'As always, she knew better than to waste an opportunity...' 'It cost her nothing...' And through the eyes of her audience. Their attitude to Anthea shows how much they respect and admire her. It would have been difficult to relay this information through my heroine's own point of view without having her seem immodest: 'Anthea could see how much they admired her; she knew they looked up to her...'

Physical description is another essential part of exposition. Having Anthea seen from her audience's viewpoint allows the scene to serve several purposes—not only describing her but further emphasizing her effect on her admirers.

Description is best kept brief and selective. Instead of presenting it all in one large block, it is best slotted in over the course of several paragraphs.

Keep in mind that when exposition looks exactly like what it is—feeding the reader facts that are essential to the story—it detracts from the plot. In popular fiction, the reader's main interest is always the storyline.

Does your exposition work?

To test for faulty exposition, ask yourself these questions:

- Is this information essential for the reader to understand and believe in the characters and story?

- Are you positive that the viewpoint narrator would know the information he or she is imparting?

- Have you established locale and time? That is, does the reader know where and when the scene is taking place?

Middles

So you've got a great beginning. You've handled the task of exposition, introducing and describing the heroine while at the same time establishing her main conflict or problem, and you have a pretty good idea of how the story is going to end. Now what about the middle?

This is where a lot of beginner writers come to an abrupt halt. They feel daunted by the effort of imagining the incidents which must now give momentum to the story.

These middle chapters must develop the plot, building tensions, uncertainty, triumphs and suspense. At the start the heroine is faced with some terrible problem. After that, the idea is to heap complication on complication as she struggles to solve that problem.

Complications

As soon as one complication is solved, your heroine must face the next, which should always tighten the screw. The final crisis, or complication, should always be the worst. My own stories usually end with nearly everything my heroine holds dear on the line. If you have made your readers really care about your lead character, they'll be on the edge of their seats if she looks as if she's about to lose everything that's important to her.

Complications should always arise from whatever problem your heroine is facing. If you merely throw a few spanners in the works as a diversion, or to pad out your story, this weakens your storyline. What you are creating are not complications but hindrances or delays that will merely irritate your readers.

Complications work best when they arise naturally from what has gone before. This means using cause and effect. You should aim to have one crisis lead logically to another, instead of merely imagining a sequence of random events. For example:

Complication 1:

Your heroine is stumped by a witness who refuses to speak. The witness changes his mind when he finds his life is under threat. He rings the heroine and leaves a garbled message on her answering machine. The heroine, relieved, rushes to the witness's house.

Complication 2:

Heroine arrives to find the witness murdered. But you give the story a chance to develop by having her work out the clues in the garbled message.

Whatever you decide on as complications, these are best solved by your heroine's *actions* rather than by relying on coincidence, good luck, or too much outside help.

For example, instead of having our heroine, Kate, just happen to find the villain's incriminating letter, which blows out of his open car window, you have an opportunity to emphasize her resourcefulness and nerve by letting her find a way in to the villain's office after hours and risk discovery in going through his files.

In this way you show your heroine taking an active role, which should *always* be your aim, while at the same time the threat of discovery adds to the suspense.

Endings

The end of your story is every bit as vital as the beginning. The way you solve your heroine's problems and tie up the loose ends determines the final impression you will leave with your readers and whether or not they will be eager to read your next novel. How many good stories have you read that promised so much yet had such weak and contrived endings that you threw the book away in disgust? This applies to movie criticism, too.

As I've said, some writers know exactly how they are going to end their stories before they start. Others have only a vague idea. I do think it's important to have at least some idea of how you're going to solve the heroine's problems before you begin. As we're dealing here with popular fiction, a happy ending, or a strong suggestion of one, is preferable. If you are scornful about such a contrivance, perhaps you should take another look at the work of the authors who make the most money! Happy endings are what readers of popular fiction expect. If you want to sell your story you should meet the readers'—and the publisher's—expectations.

This isn't to say that tragedies can't occur, or that the heroine can't lose people close to her. Kill off the heroine at the end, however, and you'll probably kill off your chances of being published.

In deciding on a solution to your heroine's problems, you should make sure that it is in keeping with all the pages of tension and build-up that have gone before. A solution that could have been accomplished much earlier, or one that depends on coincidence or improbable strokes of luck, is going to leave your readers unconvinced and dissatisfied.

Another thing to remember when writing your final scene is to ensure that your main character is actively involved. At this vital point in the story, your heroine should always be on stage.

As the climax approaches, the action should gather pace. This isn't the time to introduce new characters or launch into lengthy description that might slow the action or distract from the final crisis.

Once that point is reached, your aim should be to end your story as quickly as possible. The most that should be required at this stage is a page or two to tie up loose ends and give the reader a chance to catch her breath after the tension and excitement of the climax. Too much rambling leads to a sense of anticlimax—which can sometimes come about when writers find themselves so attached to their characters that they're loath to end their story.

If your story has the potential for further development, maybe you can write a whole new novel! But don't try artificially to manipulate the ending just because you have a vague idea for a sequel. A story that ends inconclusively is unsatisfying to most readers and certainly won't tempt them to rush out and buy your next work.

Some stories end in surprise twists. If you have this in mind, you must lay the groundwork carefully earlier in your story. The trick at that stage is not to be so heavy-handed you give the twist away. Weave in just enough hints to make the outcome plausible. Again, you can learn how this is done by studying writers who do it well.

Flashback

Telling your reader about past events is exposition. Dramatizing them in a scene or scenes is flashback.

The reason for using flashback is usually to enable you to start at a dramatic point (using a flash forward, in other words) and so grab your readers' attention. Then, using flashback, you can go back and fill in all the relevant detail. A flash forward is often set off from the rest of the novel as a prologue. Where a novel's final chapter jumps ahead in time from the climactic point of the story (another flash forward, really), this can similarly be labelled an epilogue.

If you start your novel with a flash forward, you might show your character at a moment of crisis in her adult life. From there, you can flashback to her childhood and continue the story chronologically until you reach the point at which you began.

In *Indecent Ambition*, I begin with my heroine in the present and break off at a very dramatic point into a flashback that fills in her background and explains her motivation. Then I pick up the story again at the dramatic opening moment and continue the storyline chronologically to the end.

Flashback disrupts a story's time sequence, so it is important to ensure that the present-time storyline is strongly established before you split off into the past.

Flashback should not be used to pad out a thin storyline. What you decide to reveal in flashback must have direct relevance to the story's present. That is, learning about the heroine's past should help your readers to understand what is driving her present actions.

If you use too many lengthy flashbacks to fill in the backgrounds of a number of different characters, you risk confusing your readers. Remember, not everything that happens in the past needs to be reported in a long, drawn-out flashback. Sometimes all that is needed is a single line of past dialogue. Alternatively, the information you wish to relate can be given in exposition.

For a flashback to be effective it must have all the drama and vitality of the present-time story. Although set in the past, it also needs action, character development, dialogue and conflict. A flashback is really a story within a story.

Exercise 2

Without trying to develop a whole storyline, write three or four of the most intriguing opening sentences you can think of. Then expand each of them into half a dozen paragraphs which contain some exposition of character, time and place.

Chapter 6: I Couldn't Put It Down!

Handling pace, suspense and background

Popular fiction depends for its appeal on a fast-moving plot, but a story can't continue at breakneck speed. Too much exciting action without any let-up can be as off-putting as lack of action. It's important to offer resting points between the peaks of the various crises so readers can catch their breath.

These 'breathers' are necessary to give your overall work an effective rhythm. There are various ways to slow the pace of your narrative. They include using exposition or description, changing points of view, or picking up the threads of the sub-plot.

Crises and lulls must be carefully balanced—the lulls not too drawn-out, the crises not coming on top of one another. You need to avoid a story in which all the dramatic action occurs in the first six chapters. At the same time the lulls, no matter how gentle, must always contain the seeds of the next crises. As your story comes to an end the momentum should increase.

Another technique which helps to pace your story is the leap in time. This allows you to bridge the gaps between incidents without tediously detailing every step of the action in between.

For example, you might write a dramatic scene of confrontation between the heroine and another character which ends in the heroine deciding to return to the small country town where she grew up in the hope of discovering some truth. In this case there is no need to describe her packing for the journey, asking the neighbor to feed the cat, or buying her ticket! There is not even any need to describe the journey itself. Your very next scene can simply show your character arriving in the town. And you can use the same scene as an opportunity for more exposition.

Let's say, for example, that your heroine arrives hot and thirsty and enters a local cafe for a drink. This affords a 'lull' in which you can explore her thoughts about her situation and what her next step might be. Alternatively, you could have her remembering the last time she was in the town, which can lead naturally into a flashback that fills the reader in on the heroine's background.

Perhaps it could happen like this:

> The heavy, lank-haired waitress put the milkshake down in front of her without a smile. It wasn't until she walked away that Maggie realized who it was.
>
> God... Tina Clark. They'd sat next to each other in sixth grade. Maggie remembered how envious she'd been of Tina's dark, fat curls, her budding breasts. Casting a sideways glance at the sullen-faced woman who stood behind the fly-marked counter, she saw there was nothing to envy now. Tina Clark's youth had been wasted in Lewisville. Her future was as predictable as it was bleak.
>
> Maggie looked away as the other girl turned and caught her gaze. But there was no flicker of recognition in those dull, weary eyes. Maggie knew she was safe. The skinny, nervous kid who had been Marguerite Benson was long since gone. She'd made sure of that.
>
> But in the hot stupor of that Lewisville noon, she found herself remembering the days when all she had thought of was escape, when her obsession had been to create a future that would erase forever the shame of her past.

This scene not only leads very naturally into flashback, but also throws out a 'lure'. By arousing curiosity about what might have happened in Maggie's past you encourage the reader to keep turning the pages.

In the next example, taken from *Never Forget Me*, my aim is to build tension and then change pace by skipping into flashback. I end one chapter like this:

As the gates began to swing open he stepped on the gas, shooting the Lincoln over the curb, half blocking the E-Type's access to the drive beyond.

He saw her startled expression as he threw open his door. 'Tess! Tess, it is you, isn't it?' He tapped on the driver's window.

Tess stared transfixed into the face she had never forgotten. A face from another time, another place.

'Nick...' she breathed.

Oh God.

The next chapter begins:

The child waited till she was sure they were asleep...

This becomes a flashback into Tess's background that tells how and when and in what circumstances she met Nick. I fill in the necessary details for a number of chapters, then bring the reader back to the present with Nick and Tess sitting over their drinks, their reminiscing complete.

Suspense: Go on, be a tease

Pacing and suspense are inextricably linked because a story is made up of a number of crises, each building up to the denouement. But suspense isn't generated by pages of violent action such as fights or car chases. Rather it comes from keeping readers in a state of worry and fear about characters *they really care about*. There should always be some risk to the major character and this risk should always arise from her struggle to reach her goal.

At the same time, however, it's not a good idea to place your heroine in situations in which she is continually defeated, because then you're more likely to depress than thrill your readers. By allowing your main character small victories, you add to the general suspense because the reader is never sure if this time the heroine will pull it off or not. Whenever she does, her success helps to make her final triumph more credible.

Another way to tease and tantalize is only to tell your readers what is absolutely necessary. **Suspense is created by hinting at the crisis to come and by withholding information from the reader until the last possible moment.**

Here is another example from *Never Forget Me:*

> A tight-faced Adelle switched off the television and drew deeply on her cigarette. As she began to pace the room she blew out an angry stream of smoke.
>
> 'We've got to stop this, Dave!' she hissed, the tendons standing out like strands of rope on her thin neck. 'I don't give a damn now what happened between Tom and her but that slut's not going to be allowed to wreck things for me from beyond the grave.'
>
> Larry Brandt and Dave Arnell exchanged nervous looks. If Adelle only knew that it was so much more than that.

The last line provides the hook. As the next scene focuses on another character, to satisfy their curiosity readers are forced to read on. This is how you give a storyline momentum.

Suspense works through anticipation or foreshadowing. By laying down hints and clues about some exciting or dramatic event to come you keep the reader turning the pages. To plant these clues effectively you need to have a very clear idea about the next dramatic event you are heading towards. Only then can you know what background you have to establish, what characters you're going to need, and so on.

This example comes from *A Very Public Scandal:*

That night Charles found sleep difficult. It was a problem that had begun to plague him with increasing frequency.

Restless, he kicked off the sheet and, dressed only in shorts, threw open the French doors to his small bedroom patio.

A low golden moon hung over the park. The noises of the city were stilled. He leaned against the scrolled patio rail, feeling the cold of the metal against his bare flesh. Panic bubbled in his throat and he experienced the now familiar churning in his belly.

Oh God. His hands gripped like vices around the railing. What was he going to do?

What was he going to do?

Suspense here comes from giving the reader no hint about what is troubling Charles. It is knowing that something is going to happen but not knowing when or how that keeps the reader on the edge of her seat. But you won't win readers if you cheat. If I had failed to follow up on what was worrying Charles, or if I had later revealed that he was worried merely because he'd forgotten to buy his wife a birthday present, my readers would be more than justified in tossing my story aside. As Chekhov insisted, if there is a gun in Chapter 1 then in some later chapter that gun must be fired. In other words, don't set up expectations that you don't or can't fulfil.

Suspense is also created when characters do the unexpected. Readers usually like to guess what is going to happen next so a twist that catches them by surprise will add to their enjoyment of the story.

Another way of generating suspense is to establish a time limit within which your major character must solve her problem. For example, an American lawyer might have only 48 hours to save her innocent client from the electric chair. Or the hero might have just three days to discover the details of the assassination plot, or 24 hours to find where the terrorists have planted a bomb.

Creating suspense is one of the aspects of writing I enjoy most. I love to keep my readers guessing, and when I'm told my novels are almost impossible to put down, I know I've succeeded. The technique of carry-over suspense is a good way to keep readers turning the pages. By ending a chapter with an irresistible hook I make sure they will find it impossible to put the story aside!

Here are some of those suspenseful chapter endings:

> *... Louisa is the only reason I'm going to talk about something I've never told another soul.*
>
> And:
>
> *Tess picked up the receiver. 'Paula, what's up? Is something wrong?'*
>
> *A chill ran through her as she listened to the other woman's rapid explanation.*

The use of carry-over suspense is another aspect of the technique of withholding information for as long as possible.

Problems in handling suspense

Too much of a good thing can always be a mistake, and this goes for suspense too. Care must be taken not to drag out intrigue on too many fronts for too long. If you try to keep all your balls in the air at the same time you'll end up irritating rather than intriguing your readers. You can avoid this by resolving one issue before going on to raise new questions.

Another common error in handling suspense is to write something like this: 'If Rosemary had known what was going to happen, she would never have gone to Oldmoor House that day.' This heavy-handed way of trying to engender anticipation in the reader is outmoded, amateurish and best avoided.

The structure of your novel—where you decide to slot in your highs and lulls—is also very important in sustaining tension.

When planning your storyline, if you put your most dramatic scene at the halfway point whatever follows can only be anticlimactic.

This doesn't mean that you have to discard what might be an intriguing plot. But you're going to have to do a lot more hard thinking about how best to structure your plot so that the biggest climax comes where it should—at the end.

Setting, background, atmosphere

Your choice of setting will obviously depend on your characters and story, but setting can also be used to evoke atmosphere.

Just think of the differences between stories set on a lonely, mist-shrouded island off the coast of Scotland, in a hot and dusty outback town, or in the sophisticated bustle of Paris or New York.

Whichever background you decide on, your task is to evoke it as clearly as possible in the reader's mind. This doesn't mean writing pages of description. It can take only a few well-considered lines to sketch in a background. But often a beginner writer isn't quite sure what to put in and what to leave out.

A good idea is to close your eyes and imagine the scene in your mind. Image the street, house, room, or whatever and try to see the details as well as the overall picture. Then pick out the most telling aspects: a wonderful lamp, the lingering odor of tobacco or the heavy scent of fresh flowers, the layers of dust on a piano, a garish mass-market print, the rumble of nearby traffic. Select whatever will make the most evocative impression on your readers. In describing a wealthy businessman's home you might mention only three or four items—an antique table, chandeliers, a grand piano, the park-like setting through the French windows. But this is enough. Your readers will paint the rest of the picture themselves. Similarly, if you're trying to draw a shabby apartment shared by young inner-city types you might refer to the rock posters on the wall, the mismatched chairs, the clutter of newspapers and unwashed dishes, the bicycle at the end of the hall. An effectively sketched setting always reveals more about your characters.

Here are a couple of examples from *Never Forget Me*:

> Rainbow Glen was a complex of about three dozen apartments with a shabby, neglected air. Dusty oleanders dotted the patchy lawn surrounding an old-fashioned swimming pool. As he walked past the murky water Chris decided it looked capable of producing a whole new world of deadly diseases.

The chief impression I am trying to convey here is one of shabbiness and decay.

Another example:

> The first thing he noticed was the overwhelming stench—a mixture of cats and stale booze. The blinds were pulled down tightly over each window and it took his eyes a moment to adjust to the dimness... Three cats leapt aside as he lowered himself onto the ancient sofa.

I use the description of the room to tell the reader about the character who lives there. It's more subtle than writing, 'Suzie Hawkins lived alone in a shabby apartment. She was a cat-lover with a weakness for liquor.'

On a larger scale, this extract from *A Very Public Scandal* shows how I sketch in the background of Australia, in particular Sydney, in the 1950s:

> Over the next few weeks Marianne felt her senses bombarded by myriad impressions of the strange and exotic country that was to be her home. The stifling summer heat, the glare, the colors and scents of unfamiliar blossoms and trees, the stunning spectacle of

Saturday afternoon sails on the harbor—all intrigued her.

Sydney, too, with its trams and ferries and busy streets, had its own particular charm. While the city might have lacked the sophistication of London, the people, she decided, were among the friendliest on earth—even if the slow, drawling accents of some occasionally eluded her.

It takes just a few lines to convey the important details. I wanted my readers—especially the foreign ones—to feel the heat, smell the exotic foliage, see the harbor, the glare and colors, hear the accents. Most importantly, I give no details about the flora—my character is a foreigner and wouldn't be expected to know such information.

Another point to remember about backgrounds is the need to avoid setting too many scenes in the one place. Vary your locations so that your heroine is seen in different surroundings—her place of work, her home, restaurants, shopping, the beach, her lover's apartment, her parents' home, and so on. This adds interest to your story and also offers the opportunity to develop your character more fully.

Bear in mind that the more authentically you draw your background, the more credibility you establish with your readers. But take care not to overuse the details you've amassed in your research into background or setting. Just because you know everything it's possible to know about St Petersburg, you don't have to include all that information in your novel. Most readers of popular fiction are looking for a story, not a travelogue, so select only those details that are necessary and interesting. And as with character description, background detail should be woven into the storyline a little at a time rather than delivered in one solid lump.

The next two examples from *Whisper Her Name* show how little detail I needed to set my scene in Paris both in the present and just after the Second World War. In neither case have I made any reference to the Eiffel Tower!

As he sipped at his espresso he watched the passers-by on the Rue de Rivoli. It was the end of September and the tourist barbarians were almost gone. Once more the city belonged to the Parisians.

And:

While Paris still carried the scars of its fight for liberty, the city had quickly resumed its joie de vivre. The tourists were back, the restaurants were busy, the cabarets as risqué as ever. As well, the hotels were full of serious-faced businessmen eager to capitalize on the potential of markets too long disrupted by the irritation of war.

If you want to use a background with which you still don't feel entirely familiar, one technique is to write the story from the point of view of an outsider coming to the place for the first time. This way your heroine can't be expected to have an intimate knowledge of the area—and hopefully your credibility remains intact!

To write concise description that effectively evokes background and setting takes effort but, like most tasks, it gets easier with practice.

Chapter 7: Who's Talking? Who's Thinking?

Dialogue

A few lines of good dialogue can do more to bring your story to life than pages of narrative. **Dialogue serves three main purposes: it reveals character, advances the story, and provides necessary information.**

Nothing does quite so much to create believable, well-rounded characters as effective dialogue. The words you put into your characters' mouths should help to reveal mood, personality and emotional state. This can be achieved not only through the words themselves but through your description of facial expression, gestures and mannerisms.

Take this example: 'Mary died this morning,' he said with a smile. Words that we expect to be spoken with regret are given a whole new meaning by the description of the speaker's incongruous facial expression; this helps to reveal much about the character.

But dialogue as it is used in a novel can never replicate natural speech. If you included all the repetitions, contradictions, interruptions and half-finished sentences that are typical of the way most of us communicate, readers would very quickly be bored stiff. For the same reason, writers never put down everything a character would really say in the given circumstances. The most obvious example is the social niceties. When character A rings character B with an important message it is pointless to bother with the conventional greetings: 'Good morning, Tim,' 'Good morning, Julia.' 'How are you?' 'Fine, thanks.'

Instead you should come right to the point, keep the storyline moving, and reveal more about the characters:

'Tim? It's Julia. It want you in this office at three sharp.'

At the other end of the line Tim Wilson could barely control his temper. 'Can't be done, I'm afraid. Got a meeting across town at two-thirty.'

'I said three sharp.' She hung up.

When writing dialogue for your various characters it is essential to keep in mind their age, background and education—a middle aged woman is going to talk very differently from a teenager, a priest very differently from a laborer. If you look at all the following ways to say 'yes' you'll realize how choice of dialogue underlines character type: 'sure', 'certainly', 'okay', 'yep', 'sure thing', 'okey dokey', 'of course', 'my pleasure', 'yeah'.

Dialogue always has to be tailored to fit the person speaking. But don't forget that how someone speaks can also be determined by whom they are addressing. The way people talk to peers and family is bound to be different from the way they communicate with superiors or authority figures. When you use dialogue to reveal these differences you give greater insight into a character's personality.

If you've done your homework and know your characters well, their speech will also reveal their emotional reaction to people and situations. For example, a character who is bombastic and outgoing will react very differently from one who is more diffident and withdrawn. If you were writing a confrontation between one of these characters and a colleague the former might say, *'Oh, come on, Tony, you can't be serious! That's asking for trouble.'* The latter, on the other hand, would be more likely to respond, *'Do you really think that's the way to handle this, Tony?'*

It may be stating the obvious to write that dialogue should be 'speakable'. But too many novice writers produce dialogue that is merely narrative set in quotation marks. Compare these examples:

The new manager could not contain her wrath. 'I have no intention of sharing an office! If it is not possible for me to be given a room of my own than I have no option but to offer my resignation without delay. I will not be treated like an inferior.'

And:

The new manager exploded. 'You can't be serious! I'm not sharing an office! I get a place of my own or I'm walking out right now. No one's going to treat me like some second-rate junior!'

The first example is formal and far too stilted. The second is much more realistic. However, if you wanted to portray your character as stiff and pedantic, the first example would suit. It's always a matter of tailoring the words to the speaker.

In the next pair of examples you can see how the choice of words paints two totally different character types:

'Please come in. You look absolutely exhausted. Take a seat and I'll get you a cup of tea.'

And:

'Come in love... Hell, you look totally pooped.. Take the weight off your feet and I'll get you a cuppa.'

Some occupations—journalism, sailing, medicine and so on—have a jargon of their own and this too can be used to help flesh out your characters. But avoid being too heavy-handed. An odd word here or there is all that is required to indicate a particular profession or background. Too much jargon gets in the way of the story and can confuse and irritate your readers.

Another mistake is to try to reproduce accents or dialect phonetically: 'I 'ope zees ees not too 'ot for you.' Instead, use syntax to imply the foreignness of the character: 'The tea? It is not too hot for you?'

Another simple way to give the impression of a foreign accent is merely to eliminate contractions. Use 'I will' or I cannot' instead of 'I'll' and 'I can't'.

A special manner of speaking can also be indicated outside the dialogue. *"What is your name?" His German accent was almost impenetrable.* Or: *'I really can't understand why such people bother to come here.' The woman's upper-class bray made Anne squirm.*

Another way to handle accent or special speech is to start with a modified phonetical version and then continue in plain English.

In this example from *Indecent Ambition* I use mainly syntax to remind the reader of my character's Irish background:

> Nan's pale blue eyes glistened at the memory. 'Keen as mustard I was to learn to dance. My poor mother couldn't say no to the likes of me. Somehow she was findin' the money and off I went to classes. Miss Valmay was her name, the teacher. And no nonsense did that one take; tough as a sergeant major she was ... There were twelve of us in that class, but only me, mind, with the drive and determination to be tryin' for the big time...'

Nan's speech indicates her age and her Irish heritage and at the same time provides information about her background and character. This type of exposition is always far more popular with readers than pages of narrative.

The alternative, which would not have worked nearly as well, might have read like this:

> *The two women spent the afternoon deep in conversation. Nan told Lenore about her childhood in Ireland, about her love of dancing, and how she had pestered her mother to allow her to attend dancing classes with a Miss Valmay who, Nan chuckled, had been as tough as a sergeant major.*

Dialogue is a much more interesting vehicle for this information and also reveals more of Nan's personality. The words I put in her mouth make her persistence and determination clear.

Here, from *A Very Public Scandal* is another example of dialogue revealing character:

> Edwina Rolfe paid her first visit to the house not long after they moved in. Ignoring her daughter-in-law, she directed her comments at her son as she inspected the new abode.
>
> 'Can't see how you can live without a water view, Charles. Surely you could have found something on the harbor to suit?'
>
> 'This is the place we liked best, Mother,' Charles answered evenly. 'The view of the park is almost like living in the country.'
>
> Raising a haughty eyebrow, his mother murmured. 'All right for those who like the country, I suppose...'
>
> 'Will you stay for afternoon tea, Mrs Rolfe?' Marianne was leading the way towards the sunroom that overlooked the rear garden. 'I've had the housekeeper make–'
>
> 'Not today, I'm afraid.' Edwina Rolfe was pulling on her gloves. She kissed Charles, nodded at her daughter-in-law.
>
> 'I'd rip up that awful carpet if I were you,' were her parting words as she slid into the rear seat of the car.

Note that whenever a new character speaks it is important to start a new paragraph. This is the case even if the character says only one word. Also, note that putting Edwina's final words in a separate paragraph from her previous ones helps indicate the lapse of time between her leaving the house and getting into her car.

If you have created a character whose normal mode of speech would be ungrammatical, don't be afraid to reflect this in your writing:

> *'Get outta here! And don't come back! I don't know nothin' d'you hear? I've forgotten everything about that night!'*

The character's status and background are immediately clear.

Strong language, too, may be needed for certain characters. An ex-con is hardly likely to say 'Oh, dear' when he gets one on the nose during a fight! If you are uncomfortable with the actual words, an alternative might be to write: *'Frank swore under his breath.'* Or: *'A stream of foul language followed her out of the courtroom.'*

One of the best ways to check for faulty or stilted dialogue is to read your words aloud. Recording them can also be a great help. By listening to yourself speak your characters' words you will pick up such mistakes as 'I cannot', 'she will', 'he will not' and so on. These sound much more natural as 'I can't', 'she'll', 'he won't'.

Remember in school when we had to make lists of all the words we could think of that could be used instead of 'said'? Proudly we filled columns with 'exclaimed', 'replied', 'stated', demanded', 'murmured', 'grunted', and so on. Well, it's my sad task to tell you that using streams of substitute attributives throughout your writing is the sign of an amateur.

> *'I'm going!' he fumed.*
>
> *'No you're not,' she retorted.*
>
> *'Are you trying to tell me what to do?' he demanded.*

There is absolutely nothing wrong with 'said'. Simple and unobtrusive, it can be slipped into your writing without disrupting the flow of dialogue. This isn't to say that you can't add variety occasionally—but make sure it is just occasionally.

If I ever use a word other than 'said' it is usually only to indicate *how* something is spoken. For example:

'Don't go,' she murmured.

'I hate her,' she whispered.

'It hurts,' she moaned.

Be careful, too, not to attach an adverb or adverbial phrase to your attributive verb if the meaning is already clear:

'Leave me alone!' she screamed angrily.

'Don't leave me,' she sobbed tearfully.

'I love you,' he whispered softly.

An excellent device for breaking up a fairly lengthy exchange between two characters is to use what are sometimes called tag lines. These lend variety and colour to a piece of dialogue and help bring the scene to life. The first example uses attributives, the second employs tag lines that convey only the action:

'Yes, Clare,' he said, tapping the letter in front of him, 'they want me.'

'Oh, Bob!' she exclaimed as she threw her arms around his neck. 'That's wonderful!'

'Yes, Clare,' he tapped the letter in front of him. 'They want me.'

'Oh, Bob!' She threw her arms around his neck. 'That's wonderful!'

Another example:

'Oh, Mike...' She couldn't hide her fear. 'Are they going to be able to save it?'

'They're doing their best. Tess.' His voice was flat. 'Let's get the hell outta here and leave them to it.'

The alternative might be:

'Oh, Mike...'she said fearfully, 'are they going to be able to save it?'

'They're doing their best, Tess,' he answered flatly...

There is nothing wrong with this last version. But tag lines can be very useful in dialogue to add variety and to keep a scene dynamic. Here are some more examples:

'You don't expect me to believe that!' Her eyes were scornful.

She smiled bitterly. 'I was the last to know.'

Her voice softened. 'Please... take me with you.'

'Don't move!' His grip tightened on her arm.

'Are you sure?' She choked back a sob.

'No, I wasn't there.' She avoided his eyes as she told the lie.

'Well, you stay if you like.' He headed for the door. 'But I'm going.'

He smacked his thigh. 'I've got it!'

The next examples illustrate how long tracts of dialogue can be eliminated when the information being imparted doesn't have to be spelt out in speech:

'But how do you know about John Lang?'

She told him then about meeting the businessman on the flight to Melbourne, about his interest in her project and his offer of a place on the team.

'And you accepted?'

Sara nodded. 'Yes. It was too good a chance to miss.'

And:

Her voice broke. 'Oh, Father, I just don't know what I'm going to do. I can't afford...'

At the other end of the line the priest did his best to comfort her.

Here, narrative is used to avoid long-winded dialogue that will only bore readers.

Sometimes beginner writers are so involved with getting the dialogue right they forget to tell their readers where the conversation is taking place. Here is how to slip such information in unobtrusively:

'Are they going to do it?' She kept her voice low although they had the patio to themselves.

He gave her a long look. 'Yes, tomorrow. When he leaves the office.'

Or:

They met at a small coffee lounge in George Street. He saw her wave from the back of the room.

'Sorry I've kept you.' He pulled out a seat.

Impatiently, she waved away his apologies. 'What happened?'

Haltingly Nick passed on the bad news and saw her eyes fill with tears.

This last line also demonstrates how to relay to a character information the reader has already been told. A really important short cut that saves boring the reader.

Exercise 3

Read the three passages below. Which makes the most effective use of dialogue?

1.

Sara made her way to John Kelly's office. Taking a deep breath, she knocked on the door.

'Come in.' Her colleague sounded as if he didn't want to be disturbed.

His tone changed at once when he saw who it was. Immediately he was on his feet, ushering her inside.

'Sara… what a lovely surprise… take a seat.'

'I'm sorry to disturb–' she began as she took the chair he offered.

'Not at all.' He waved away her apologies. 'Just tackling the usual problem—trying to make our PM sound more intelligent than he is.'

'Not an easy task.'

'You said it. But that's what they pay me for… Can I offer you a drink? There's scotch, or vodka, if you'd prefer.'

'No thanks, John.' She could feel the clamminess of her palms.

'Something else then? A glass of wine?'

Sara spoke through dry lips. 'John, this isn't a social call. I need your help.'

John Kelly was looking at her, his grey brows drawn together. 'Something's the matter, Sara. What is it?'

She swallowed hard. 'There's three million dollars missing from the Jackson account.'

2.

> Taking a deep breath, Sara knocked on John Kelly's door.
>
> Her colleague greeted her warmly. 'Sara… what a lovely surprise, take a seat. Can I get you a drink?'
>
> 'John—this isn't a social call.'
>
> He shot her a quick appraising look. 'What is it, Sara? What's happened?'
>
> She forced the words from her dry lips. 'Something terrible. There's three million dollars missing from the Jackson account.'

3.

> Sara knew she had to tell someone. She knocked on John Kelly's door.
>
> 'Come in.'
>
> As she entered, her colleague greeted her warmly.
>
> 'Sara… what a lovely–'
>
> She cut across him. 'John, listen to me. There's three million dollars missing from the Jackson account.'

There is nothing really wrong with the first example if John Kelly is going to play an important part in the story. If not, then you could cut a lot of the unnecessary rambling. The third example, on the other hand, is so brief that you lose the chance to make any real emotional impact.

Viewpoint

One of the vital decisions you will have to make before you begin to write concerns viewpoint. In other words, through whose eyes is the story going to be told? The answer will determine whether you are going to enter into the thoughts and feelings of just one character or more than one. **Even when a story has several 'viewpoint' characters, one of them usually stands out as the main character.**

In popular fiction there are usually three choices regarding viewpoint:

- first person
- third person from the viewpoint of one character only, and
- third person from the viewpoint of several characters.

First person

A story written in the first person takes the viewpoint of 'I', the narrator, throughout. An advantage of using first person is that it can give a greater illusion of reality by helping readers to identify with the viewpoint character.

But there are disadvantages too, in that we can see or hear only what 'I' sees or hears and know only 'I's' private thoughts. For this reason the first person viewpoint can make it necessary to use clumsy plot devices. For example, you may have to put your viewpoint character in a position where she can 'overhear' information which is essential for the development of the plot.

Yet another drawback can be the monotony of having to repeat 'I' throughout the story. In third person viewpoint you have the choice of using the character's name—Tom, say,—the appropriate pronoun, he, or other alternatives such as the man, the teacher and so on.

Let's look at an example of first person viewpoint:

I was still reeling from the shock of the news. 'Can I get you a drink?' Peter was looking at me with sympathy.

I shook my head. 'No...' I never could understand how alcohol was supposed to soothe a heavy heart.

He put a hand on my shoulder. 'What about if I ring Dr Allen?'

I managed to force out the words. 'Please, I'll be all right.' At that moment all I wanted was to be left alone.

The next example demonstrates faulty first person viewpoint:

I took a seat next to Jim Mason. He felt his pulses race. He thought I was going to make a pass at him.

There is no way the narrator, 'I', could have known that Jim 'felt his pulses race'. Not could 'I' know that Jim thought 'I' was going to make a pass at him.

Third person single viewpoint

In using the third person—he or she—you have the choice of entering the thoughts and feelings of just one character (third person restricted, or single, viewpoint) or of more than one character (multiple viewpoint).

Telling your story in the third person from the viewpoint of one character has similar limitations to the use of the first person. Your viewpoint character must see or hear or be told about everything and your readers can only enter into that character's thoughts. Here's an example:

Her head spun. She was still reeling from the shock of the news.

'Can I get you a drink?' Peter was looking at her with sympathy.

Jane shook her head. 'No.' She had never understood how alcohol was supposed to soothe a heavy heart.

He put his hand on her shoulder. 'What about if I ring Dr Allen?'

She managed to force out the words. 'Please. I'll be all right.' At that moment all she wanted was to be left alone.

Third person multiple viewpoint

Telling a story in the third person from the viewpoints of several characters avoids the technical difficulties of the first two methods. Readers can enter the minds of several characters and know what they are thinking and feeling. Other characters in the story are observed from the outside by the viewpoint characters.

There are a few important rules to remember about using multiple viewpoints. **As close as possible to the beginning of your story you must establish that several viewpoints are going to be used so that readers know to expect it.**

Once you have done this, you must use multiple viewpoints consistently from then on. It would be a mistake to use multiple viewpoints in Chapters 1 to 3 and then to stick with a single viewpoint. Here's an example of how to handle third person, multiple viewpoint narration:

'Can I get you a drink?' Peter was looking at her with sympathy.

Jane shook her head. She had never understood how alcohol was supposed to soothe a heavy heart.

Peter felt useless. He put a hand on her shoulder. 'What about if I ring Dr Allen?'

She managed to force out the words. 'Please. I'll be all right.' At that moment all she wanted was to be left alone.

As he looked at the pain in those beautiful dark eyes, Peter wished that he'd been the one to die.

In this example we know the thoughts of both characters. Only Peter knows that he wishes he could have been the one to die, so we can learn that only through his viewpoint.

Here is another example:

'Do you know what this will do to your father? After all the sacrifices he's made?' Anne Lewis was filled with anger and disappointment as she faced her seventeen-year-old son. She felt like slapping his face. Mike's dream had been to see Paul take his degree.

'I did my best.' Paul mumbled, averting his gaze from his mother's angry face. It was a lie and he knew it. He'd only coasted along. And meeting Jeanie hadn't helped.

Anne's viewpoint: Only she would know she was filled with anger and disappointment. Only she would know that she felt like slapping her son's face.

Paul's viewpoint: Only he knows he is lying. Only he knows that meeting Jeanie was part of the reason he failed.

Beginner writers often make the mistake of changing viewpoint in the same paragraph:

Mrs Jones watched as Suzie went forward to accept the prize. Suzie felt dizzy with emotion. Mrs Jones knew she had worked so hard and deserved to win.

In this example, Mrs Jones is the viewpoint character and cannot know how Suzie is feeling. Here is how the passage should have been written:

> *Mrs Jones watched as Suzie went forward to accept the prize. She could see the glow of delight on the girl's face.*
>
> *On the dais Suzie shook the principal's hand as she accepted her prize. It was the moment she had dreamed of and no one would know how much it had cost her.*

This shows how to handle multiple viewpoints properly. We have Mrs Jones' viewpoint in one paragraph and in a separate paragraph we go into Suzie's thoughts.

In handling multiple viewpoints a sense of balance is necessary. If you chop and change too frequently it makes for a fragmented story which readers can find hard to follow. It is important to establish your characters carefully at the start, making them familiar to readers before you shift viewpoint. This helps avoid confusion and makes the change in viewpoint unobtrusive.

Multiple viewpoint narration can make plotting easier by enabling you to reveal what several characters are doing and thinking. But you can still maintain suspense by not revealing everything in a character's head until it suits your purpose.

In the following example from *Never Forget Me*, I reveal a character's thoughts without giving away his secret dread:

> Walter Conroy was a frightened man.
>
> The last time he could ever remember being frightened was when he was eleven years old and waiting for his father to come home and thrash the living daylights out of him . . . Walter had felt physically sick at the thought of his father's wrath.
>
> Almost as sick as he felt now, 53 years later, as he read the letter lying before him on the magnificent cedar desk.

He couldn't believe it had come to this.

Changing viewpoint can also be used to build suspense by leaving one character at a crisis point and starting the next scene through another viewpoint.

Sometimes too you might wish to write without crediting the viewpoint to any character at all. This is known as omniscient viewpoint. This is used only rarely and sparingly throughout the narrative. This is how it appears:

> *It was another stifling summer's day. The air was hushed,*
> *the sky a burning blue.*

The following example shows how omniscient point of view is mingled with other viewpoints:

> *It was another stifling summer's day. The air was hushed,*
> *the sky a burning blue. Clare felt the sweat trickle between*
> *her shoulder blades as she strode across the lawn.*

Also:

> *It was another stifling summer's day. The air was hushed,*
> *the sky a burning blue. As I made my way across the lawn*
> *I could feel the sweat begin to trickle between my shoulder*
> *blades.*

Mastering viewpoint is not as difficult as it may appear. The best I can suggest is that you try writing in the various points of view and see which one comes most easily to you.

Exercise 4

Create a brief background and psychological profile for the following characters and, sticking consistently to that profile, use dialogue and third person single viewpoint to develop the following scenes.

Remember, you will be revealing the thoughts of only *one* of the speakers.

- A confrontation at an airline counter between a passenger and a clerk.

- A conversation between the wife and the mistress of a man who has recently died.

- A conversation between a child and the mother who gave him/her up for adoption 20 years before.

In the first one, for example, you may decide that the passenger is a businessman whose normally short fuse is exacerbated by the fact that he has just lost a very important client. Or is he an exasperated tourist feeling inadequate away from the familiarity of his home turf?

Now write the same scene from the opposite point of view. If you like, you can take the exercise a step further by writing the scene using both participants' point of view.

Chapter 8: Style and Structure

Style, structure and research

When I started my first novel I never gave a moment's thought to what style I was going to write in. I merely put words on paper and told the story that was bursting to come out.

Only as my manuscript grew did I become aware of developing my personal style or voice, a way of writing that came most naturally to me.

By the time I finished that first novel I had, without any deliberate effort, evolved the style that best suited the story I had to tell. In the novels that followed, the pattern continued: streamlined prose, fast-paced plots with the emphasis on action rather than lengthy description—yet without sacrificing the emotional development of my characters; and continual foreshadowing to ensure constant intrigue and suspense.

So is style something we already possess or can it be learned and developed?

I think it may be true to say that style is to writing exactly as it is to fashion—an expression of our originality. Just as the clothes we choose reflect our personality, so too do the words we select to tell our stories.

To continue the analogy, giving in to the dictates of fashion means slavishly imitating the latest style. Only with time and growing confidence in our own judgment do we develop our own personal fashion sense.

It's the same with writing. Of course we can admire how other writers 'do it'. We can also subconsciously absorb various other influences. The problem arises when we try too hard to adopt another author's style.

This can only lead to confusion. The longer you try to write like someone else the longer it will take you to find the voice which is uniquely your own. And it is finding your individual voice or style that helps you to grow in confidence as a writer.

Developing your own style comes mainly from continual practice of your craft, but there are three points to keep in mind:

1. Style should not be forced. It must come naturally to you so it can be handled without artificiality.

2. It must be appropriate to your material.

3. It must be acceptable to your readers.

Readers of popular fiction expect a style that is clear and easy to read. They want to be entertained, not impressed by the writer's extensive vocabulary or convoluted prose.

Essentially your readers want to know what happens next. To keep them interested, you need to move your story ahead at a fast pace, and this is best achieved by lean, efficient prose.

Don't jump to the conclusion, however, that simple prose is simple to write. Many people have great difficulty expressing exactly what they mean. Clarity and succinctness take practice.

As a beginner, the first 30 pages or so of your work are likely to reflect either no discernible style or a whole range of styles. Don't let that worry you too much at this early stage. It's when your story begins to catch fire and your confidence in your own judgment grows that you'll find yourself gradually finding your own writing voice.

Once that happens you can return to those early pages and rewrite them with much greater skill and ease. As you rewrite you'll probably find you have to cut back and prune, as overwriting is a common error with novice writers.

At the other extreme from the verbose, florid style is the flat declarative. You may have written, 'The table was set for dinner.' See how much more a vivid a picture you draw by writing, 'The long oak table gleamed with crested silver and fine Waterford flutes.'

To illustrate the difference between this and what I mean by an overwritten, fussy style, compare it with: 'The long, oak, wooden table gleamed with wonderfully crested silver, fine Waterford champagne flutes and monogrammed napkins.'

Let's see what needs to be got rid of. For one thing, if we've described the table as 'oak' there is no need to also describe it as 'wooden'. The adverb 'wonderfully' does nothing to help a reader 'see' the silver. 'Crested' is sufficient. The word 'champagne' is also superfluous: flutes are the type of glasses used for champagne. And if you want to refer to the 'monogrammed napkins' you'll have to do it in another sentence, because they can't be described as part of the 'gleaming' table.

It is style more than anything else that sets writers apart. We've all heard the dictum that there are no new plots. So why do readers keep buying books? The answer lies in the fact that familiar storylines can be given new life by writers who use words in fresh, individual ways.

Every writer's work is different because we are all shaped by our own experiences, hopes and fears, strengths and weaknesses, loves and hates. Your writing style is as unique as your fingerprints. It cannot be forced. It will only evolve as you keep practicing your craft.

Structure

Beginner writers are often not sure how long they should make their story, how many chapters it should have, how long each chapter should be.

The answer is that there are no rules. When I begin a book I only know it will be as long as I need it to be to tell my story. Your story too will find its own length as you write it.

I never know how many chapters I'm going to have or exactly how long each will be. Chapters can vary in length, but to achieve a sense of balance it helps to keep them to more or less the same number of pages. I find that an average chapter of mine comes to ten or so typed pages. However, I also use shorter chapters, focused on some vital plot development, for special effect. They certainly have impact—but not if they are overused.

Of much more importance to me as I sit down to write each day are scenes. Each of my novels appears to me as a sequence of scenes—and when I have completed what needs to be told in one set of scenes, that set becomes my chapter.

Sometimes a whole chapter is taken up with only one scene but more usually it consists of several. Different scenes don't necessarily have to involve a change of characters or location. You might open a chapter with a scene describing a married couple in a garden. The purpose of the scene is to show them having a furious quarrel. The next scene, a page or so later, might skip to lunchtime. The couple, still in the garden, are now seated with their guests and pretending a friendliness they certainly do not feel for each other.

To illustrate how you decide on scenes let's imagine you're writing a story in which a woman is eventually going to leave her husband for her lover. Here are some of the scenes you'd have to consider including:

First, you'd need to make clear the woman's unhappiness in her marriage. You could write a scene in which she asks her husband to pick her up after a late meeting. The husband's refusal because of his sporting commitments gives you plenty of scope to show the wife's reaction.

You could achieve the same effect by writing a dinner party scene in which you show the wife being belittled by her husband in front of friends.

You would need another scene to show the wife's growing attraction to the man who becomes her lover. Perhaps you could show her being impressed with his wit and intelligence as they handle a work project together. Or perhaps he is her accountant, whose gentle, supportive manner touches her when she visits him for advice.

A further scene might reveal her wrestling with her conscience, having doubts about starting the affair. The would-be lover rings her at the office, perhaps, and reluctantly she puts him off.

You wouldn't want to side-step, either, the scene in which the couple first make love. This could be used to highlight the wife's unsatisfactory sexual relationship with her husband, and/or to reveal the depth of her feelings for her lover. Then again, depending on what you want to happen in the rest of the story, you might also show her realizing she's made a big mistake!

This is a very general example. The scenes referred to could be written in a different order, and you may think of others to add. Of course, interwoven into all your scenes you also need exposition, inner monologue (the viewpoint character's thoughts), dialogue and narrative. But scene breakdowns can be a very effective tool for making a storyline more manageable.

There are other ways of making the overall structure of your novel easier to handle. One author I know uses the following plan to get started. It's not one I use myself but you may find it works for you.

She begins by writing the numbers 1 to 30 down the left-hand side of a page. These represent her chapters. Beside number 1 she jots down her ideas about a suitable opening for her story. Beside number 30 she writes how she thinks her story might end. Then beside number 2 she might write, 'introduce Kate and Steve, fill in Kate's background'. If she knows she's going to need five important characters to tell her story she decides where each of the remaining characters will be introduced. All at a party in Chapter 3? Or some in Chapter 3 and others in Chapter 5? If this is a crime story, then at number 5 she might slot in a couple of details about the first murder.

Gradually she works her way through the list of chapters, fitting in the various characters/climaxes/incidents she has decided on for her story.

At all times, however, this outline is totally flexible. Nothing is engraved in stone. Incidents and characters can be moved around to suit the development of the overall idea. As she begins to write she may realize that will be preferable to have the first murder happen in Chapter 4. Or she may decide to introduce Steve in Chapter 3 once she has dealt with the exposition for Kate in the previous chapter. Or perhaps it will add to the suspense to delay the scene in which Kate has to meet her new colleague with the fearsome reputation.

If you decide to use this method, remember that an outline is an aid to getting your story up and running. Later, its elements can be changed around as often as necessary—or even be discarded altogether.

Research

As a writer, I am always engaged in research. Every day as I read various media, watch TV, listen to people around me, read other writers' work, I am storing away facts and impressions that may be useful at some later date. Of course the greatest treasure house for writers doing research these days is the internet. Where once you might have had to drive to a library to find out various facts, now you can look up almost anything on the net. For example if you want to describe a grand English country house you can simply look up Country Life or similar magazines for ideas. Need to know something about the customs in Peru? How long it takes to get from Rome to Perugia by train? It's all there literally at your fingertips.

Of course, when setting your stories in foreign locations there is no substitute for a personal visit. First-hand experience allows you to absorb the atmosphere of a place and to observe how people behave, live, talk. And with travel being so universally affordable, even the most exotic locations may be familiar to readers. A writer can't afford to make mistakes when placing characters in foreign settings.

Since I became a writer I find I am much more observant in my travels. My senses are much more alert. A smart phone is an ideal way to capture impressions. So if I choose to locate my heroine in a specific neighborhood I carefully note what she can see from her apartment, if she can hear church bells or traffic noise, the location of the nearest supermarket, bank or newsagent. I record how long it takes her to walk to the nearest major store or subway station and even make a note of the names of the most popular neighborhood restaurants.

Remember, blatant errors can cost writers their most valuable asset—credibility.

A further shortcut to filling in location details is by way of other people's books. If, for example, you are reading a recently published story set in New York which describes the entrance to the Museum of Modern Art, take close note! That's the sort of location that's not likely to alter, and just a couple of details repeated in your own story does wonders for authenticity.

Researching your characters' personal histories can also be made easier if you read smartly. Absorbing the details of biographies, memoirs and diaries can provide you with all sorts of information about schools and education, world events at particular times, fads in dress, language, music, vacations, sports and entertainment.

Once you decide to become a writer you might never read just for pleasure again. You're always 'working'!

It is usually necessary to give some information about your characters' careers. And there are so many new areas of employment to find out about. I happen to think that writers are inherently nosy. We are curious about other human beings and that's part of the reason we write—to live in other people's skins and experience their lives. To me, this offers the best possible excuse to ask questions of my fellows.

So take the opportunities as they present themselves. Whenever you meet people who sound as if they have interesting careers, ask questions. Find out exactly what their work environment looks like, what they talk about, what gives them the pleasure/frustration in their work, even what jargon they use. In this way you will build up a store of information for future reference.

If you need to give one of your characters a profession with which you have had no contact try getting in touch with the public relations department of the appropriate company. Once you explain the reason for your interest you will almost always receive the information you want—or at least be directed to the appropriate website!

Along the same lines, it helps to have friends in the medical profession, the police force, the law and so on to call on when you need answers to your questions. I've approached my friends in various job categories many times—and they're still talking to me!

But there can be danger in research. For some would-be writers the process of filling notebooks with preparatory facts and notes is very pleasant. So much so that it becomes a way of deferring the day they start writing. Research, in other words, becomes a substitute for doing all the hard work of creation. It also saves you from putting yourself on the line and risking failure.

I've met any number of people who have been planning their novels for years but who have yet to write even the opening chapter. They prefer the *idea* of being a writer to the reality of discipline and effort.

Remember ... 'write' is an active verb.

Chapter 9: Three Pages A Day— Starting Now!

Routine, writer's block and can sex help?

If you've read this far, you are getting serious about starting that long-dreamed-of novel.

So many people think about writing. They imagine wonderful storylines, fantasize about money, fame, success, dream of how their finished book is going to look. The only thing stopping them achieving all this is having to write the damn thing!

You have studied the previous chapters closely, read other writers' work, and now feel you know enough to be confident about your ideas for a plot and characters. Every day you tell yourself: this is the day I'm going into that room, going to sit at that desk or table and *start*. Yet somehow, despite your overwhelming urge to create, the sheer magnitude of the task seems to freeze you every time.

Let me give you a suggestion to help you keep your fear under control. **What if I told you that all you had to write each day was a measly three pages? That's right—just three pages.** And what if I also said you only had to do that five days a week?

Fifteen pages a week adds up to 60 pages a month. In five to six months, then, you'll have reached your goal. Fulfilled your dream. *You will have written your first novel.* And simply by writing three pages a day. Suddenly that daunting task seems a lot more manageable, doesn't it?

Some of you, reading this, may exclaim: 'Three pages! That's nothing! I write memos—or shopping lists—longer than that!'

That's great. If you can produce more, by all means do so. But the message I am trying to convey is the value of routine. Writing eight pages twice a week isn't building the same discipline for your work as turning out three pages five days a week. And on those days when you feel tired, anxious, stressed out, 'not in the mood', you'll be far less inclined to avoid your task if you can tell yourself 'it's only three pages'.

This approach is rather like the one you need to go on a diet. The more weight you lose, the more encouraged you are to persevere. Achievement breeds resolve. With writing, the pride and fulfilment you feel in seeing that pile of manuscript pages grow makes it easier to discipline yourself to go the distance.

Getting into a writing routine is vital. Nowhere in this book have I said that writing was easy. Writing means developing the habits of discipline and determination. Every time you discipline yourself to sit down and write those three pages you make it easier to repeat the process. It'll take a week or so, but after that you'll find you are in the *habit* of working.

Some writers choose to work with music in the background but I am not one of them. I work best in total silence and solitude, and fortunately my study offers both. There have been times, however, when I have found myself enduring less than ideal conditions. While it wasn't easy, I still managed to produce my work.

If you *really* want to write you'll find a time and place to do so. And you won't allow anything to distract you. Not children, housework, personal problems or social media.

To help get yourself into the habit of writing, it's a good idea to fix on a set time every day. That may mean waking a little earlier, giving up a couple of hours of Netflix in the evening, or going to bed a little later. Only you can know at what time of day you feel most charged up and alert.

A personal routine

When I am working I stick rigidly to my daily schedule. As any of my friends will confirm, I am not a morning person. I rise early enough but wake slowly. I believe in the value of a good, filling breakfast and while I eat I also take in the day's news. I never feel guilty about the hour or so I spend doing this, as nearly all my novels have been triggered by actual events. Every day I can be sure of finding any number of ideas for future novels in news and feature stories. As I have learned never to rely on memory, I always make a note of anything of interest.

By mid-morning I am sitting at my desk, having dealt with emails and household tasks. The mere act of attending to my correspondence—business or personal—makes it easier, I find, to re-enter the creative writing mode.

The first five minutes or so are the most difficult as I set about picking up the threads of the story. I always begin by reading over the pages I have finished the night before.

Then, five minutes or so after I have begun to write, I slip easily into what can be called 'the creative coma'. Focusing intensely on the work in front of me puts me into a sort of trance which keeps all distractions at bay. I forget time and place as yet again I become totally engrossed in my characters' lives and problems.

At the end of my writing day—which is often around 1 a.m.—I note on my calendar the number of pages completed. That, and the growing thickness of my manila folder, helps give me a sense of real achievement. (Yes, having started writing at a time when computers were less reliable, I still *always* print out each day's output.) It's important, particularly when you're starting to write, to do whatever you can to boost your confidence. Noting each day's tally of pages on my calendar keeps me always trying to achieve my 'personal best' for the week or the month. Equally, a run of low numbers tells me that I've allowed too many interruptions to my working schedule.

I can't stress strongly enough the value of routine. Professional writers don't wait for something as unreliable as inspiration. It's sheer determination and force of habit—not to mention deadlines and bills!—that keep us at our task. And, of course, the joy of entering the world of the imagination. I am as keen to dive back into my characters' lives each day as I hope my readers will be when they read the completed work.

The joy of the creative process generates a wonderful momentum and no matter how tempting the invitation, I am never happy to have that momentum disturbed when I am deeply engaged in writing a novel or a screenplay. If, for however valid a reason, I am unable to sit down and write for two or more days in a row, I get edgy and nervous. I fear losing that momentum, the force of habit that turns out the pages and keeps me confident and focused. After all, writing is not the sort of job you can delegate!

When my deadlines are very tight, I work seven days a week fourteen hours or more a day. Often this is on more than one project, so I get some relief from shifting focus. At less frantic times, my schedule covers five working days of about six hours each, yet I still suffer a twinge of guilt over taking a weekend break. If anyone had told me at the beginning of my career that I could write for so long at one sitting I wouldn't have believed them. At that stage the poor little princess used to manage perhaps three or four hours before proclaiming herself exhausted!

An essential part of my writing routine involves physical exercise—yet I am well-known for my total lack of interest in sport, aerobics or gyms. Walking is my outlet. Having a dog in charge of the household ensures my adherence to this healthy and pleasant habit. Twice a day I take a   brisk walk. This is not only good for my physical well-being but also works wonders in putting the brain into that neutral state which is ideal for thinking through the next stage of my plot. More often than not I am so engrossed in my mental efforts that it is the dog who walks me. But I remain a firm believer in the maxim: *solvitur ambulando*—'the problem is solved by walking around'.

Writer's block

Even professional writers can find themselves facing a miniature writer's block as they sit down at the start of each day. This is the period when the brain has to 'warm up', as it were, when it must become nimble enough to create.

One way to get yourself started is to leave your story at the end of a working day at a point where you know exactly what is coming next. Then, when next you sit down to write, you will be confident about where you are going and excited about jumping back into the story.

Another way to get the brain into writing mode is to retype your last page or two, looking for small ways to make improvements: knocking out an adverb here, changing an adjective there, re-arranging the word order of a sentence. This trick helps to put you back into the mood you were in when your work was flowing easily the day before.

But writer's block can also occur when you are in the thick of your story. If it's a matter of a problem with the basic motivation or conflict—neither being strong or convincing enough to let you see the way ahead—then you will probably have to go back to the drawing board.

However, if the block arises from not being able to decide on the exact dialogue, for example, you can get around it by scribbling something—anything—down and putting a question mark in the margin to remind yourself to come back to this point later. The important thing is to *keep writing*.

Sometimes writer's block can be the result of self-doubt or boredom. For me, the latter usually happens on the opening pages of a new novel, and I take it as an almost unfailing signal that I am not excited enough by my plotline. Just to be sure this isn't an excuse for lazy thinking, I might worry at the passage a bit more, but if the boredom still doesn't go away I accept the fact that this particular storyline hasn't got enough going for it to sustain my passion and interest. Difficult as it is to develop a whole new plot idea, I know this is far better than persevering for another dozen pages with a storyline that is never going to catch alight.

Beginner writers are more likely to be blocked by lack of confidence. One way to overcome this is to re-read a novel you found particularly awful. You might be inspired by the thought that if such badly written stuff can get published then surely you should have an odds-on chance! I have often read that this is what encouraged dozens of now well-known writers to put pen to paper or fingers to keyboard!

The scrawl technique

Just as you don't have to have the perfect beginning before you start, it also isn't necessary to have the perfect sentence before you write. Of course you have to end up making sense to your readers, but that doesn't mean you have to start that way.

Your first task is merely to get words on paper. All these have to do is roughly express the image and ideas you have in your mind. Once you have written a page or a couple of paragraphs which capture the essence of your ideas, you will find it much easier to go back and find the best way to express what you are trying to say. Think of it like this: **first ideas, then emotions, purpose and finally, precise language.**

Once I have the basic idea for my plot, I tell the story in a series of scenes—almost exactly like a movie. **Before I begin to write a scene, I decide on its purpose,** what it needs to tell the reader. In the following example from *Never Forget Me*, my purpose was to fill in my heroine's background at the same time as I added to the intrigue:

> The sun was coming up over the San Gabriel mountains as Tess curved her way through the canyon towards her destination. There were few cars on the road and she would have enjoyed the drive had her mind not been on other things.

The tall ornate gates were already open and she drove through and stopped in the deserted car park. As she made her way slowly along the well-tended paths she noticed two workmen in the distance. It was cooler at this time of day, she supposed. Especially for their sort of work...

She didn't come here often, and it took a couple of wrong turnings before she found the place she was looking for.

Suddenly there it was in front of her. A carved marble angel, its upright wings touched by the first pink of the morning sunlight.

As motionless as a statue herself, Tess stood and looked down at the names inscribed on the pale marble slab.

Ruth and Reed Hardy

Dead almost ten years. Killed in the twin-engine aircraft her stepfather had loved to fly.

But not before Tess had learned the truth.

As she stood by the graveside, her eyes darkened with emotion, *I'm almost there*, she whispered to the ghosts around her. *Nothing is going to stop me now.*

As she'd told Nick, it was a long story...

This scene could have done the same job if I had left Tess at home in bed thinking about her past and the accident which had killed her family, or if I had used dialogue and had Tess tell the information to another character. But I saw no need to involve another character, and an interior monologue would not have had much colour or suspense.

I chose instead to *show* my heroine in an action scene and add intrigue by withholding information about where exactly the scene is set. The reader only gradually learns that Tess has arrived at a cemetery. Thus basic information is given in an interesting way, while the questions raised at the end of the scene further add to the suspense. What truth has Tess learned? What might she be stopped from doing?

In the following scene, from *Indecent Ambition*, my purpose was to introduce the wife of my villain, describe her, and indicate something of her character. I particularly wanted to show her animosity towards my heroine:

> With furious impatience Maxine Crane ripped off the crimson silk St Laurent and flung it on the floor. Shit! Five thousand dollars worth of dress and she still looked like an oversized heifer.
>
> With blazing eyes she stood in front of the full-length mirror and took in the loathsome sight of her ample body clad only in satin bra and panties. Even in the deliberate softness of her bedroom lighting the puckered, sagging flesh was clearly visible around her hips and bum. Hanging low and pendulous like two slowly leaking balloons were the large breasts she'd once flaunted so proudly. The sight made her sick...
>
> Angrily she turned away from the repulsive sight and rummaged through the rows of designer dresses in search of something that would perform the miracle of transformation.
>
> Tonight, especially, she had wanted to look her best. With Anthea James under her roof, Maxine had wanted to preen, to shine, to establish without a doubt her own status and power. Anthea James hadn't won yet.
>
> Maxine felt the anger seethe inside her. How she loathed the bitch, loathed her success, her smug self-confidence, her air of infallible righteousness.
>
> Who the hell was Anthea James after all? Where had she crawled from? For all her celebrity no one seemed to know the answer to that question. From the moment she'd burst onto the Sydney scene completely

unheralded a dozen years before, from the moment she'd opened that outrageous boutique in Double Bay, her climb had been meteoric…

Before beginning each of these scenes I asked myself what I wanted it to achieve. Then, in my mind's eye, I visualized the scene and began to *scrawl* my impressions.

I allowed the words to flow out without any restriction from my 'inner critic'. At this stage I was writing for me, not for my readers. All I wanted to do was get words on paper. They can be shaped and improved, edited and pruned later.

Etch into your mind these words: **You can't edit what you haven't written**. Make a sign of them and hang it in front of your work desk! *You can't edit what you haven't written*. Only when you have words on paper can you shape them into their final form. No writer, no matter how experienced, can bypass this process.

Creativity and inspiration

If you're waiting for inspiration, you may be waiting forever. Writing consists of talent coupled with hard work and discipline, so you shouldn't worry if it takes you a dozen starts before you finally hit on an idea that works. This is what professional writers do all the time! It is reassuring to remember that creativity is as much a process of selectivity as of coming up with ideas.

Recognizing the ideas that won't work, and why, is as important as recognizing those that will. The more effort you put into selecting ideas of value the closer you are getting to thinking like a writer. If you find creation difficult you are in good company. In all areas of creative endeavor, struggle is the norm, not the exception.

But if you stick to writing your three pages a day, five days a week, I promise you will find it easier and easier to enter the 'creative coma'. And even when you are away from your desk, you will be amazed how much work your subconscious will do for you when you are struggling with a plot problem.

But if, after prolonged effort, your story just doesn't seem to be coming together, stop trying. Creativity can't be forced, and worrying about being blocked only makes things worse. Later, when you are involved in some mundane activity like ironing, or driving, or taking a shower, the answer you are looking for will often appear as if by magic. Somehow, when the brain is in neutral, the free flow of associations solves difficulties with uncanny ease.

Getting ready for those big scenes

Some scenes in your story will be more important than others. These are scenes that can't be skipped over. They are needed at various dramatic moments and must be fully developed to capture all the colour and emotion possible.

Maybe your heroine has just found out that her business partner, a man she trusted implicitly, is working for her rivals and was responsible for her father's death. Or maybe the hero is in a fight to the death with the villain, or has just stumbled upon the body of his dead wife. On the other hand, you may be writing a scene which describes the first lovemaking between your heroine and the man she's crazy about.

These are all highly charged, emotional incidents and, as actors do, you should prepare yourself mentally to relate them—especially if the scene you are writing is not one you have experienced yourself.

I don't give much credence to the notion that you should only write what you know. I certainly don't know what it's like to kill someone, make a movie, or head a political party. But I do have a well-developed imagination! I also have an insatiable curiosity about people and what makes them behave as they do. This, I believe, is what helps me to get into my character's skin and feel what she feels. This is vital, because if a character isn't real for me, she certainly won't be real for my readers. So when I write a very dramatic and touching scene I expect to find myself as moved as I hope my readers will be.

In gearing up to write these highly charged scenes you should concentrate on attuning your own emotional state to that of your characters. Then write quickly, not worrying too much about exact words or punctuation. **Your first task is to capture the mood.**

For the same reason, I suggest you write the whole scene at one working session rather than leaving some of it for the following day. **The editing and improving can be left for another time but emotions can be difficult to recapture.** By preparing yourself mentally for the big scene, you will go a long way to overcoming the fear of writing it. And every time you conquer the fear, you will make it a little easier on yourself next time.

Is sex a dirty word?

Like those of most movies, the storylines of popular fiction nearly always include a love angle, but some beginner writers are hesitant to write about sex.

Sex is a normal part of human experience, but then so is taking a shower or cooking a meal. The point is that unless the sex scene—or shower scene, for that matter—is essential to your plot there is no need to include it. If your story is strong enough, no publisher will reject it because it 'doesn't have enough sex'.

When you write a sex scene it should help to reveal something about the two characters involved—and certainly more than we might discover if they were playing backgammon together!

For example in a sexual encounter are your characters passive? Dominant? Innocent? Experienced? Is sex something they enjoy or are they performing as a duty? Is it used to achieve other ends?

You can make the sex scene even more effective if you extend it past the act itself. This offers you the chance, through conversation or inner thoughts, to reveal a good deal about the plot or the characters.

In *Indecent Ambition* sex plays a vital role throughout. First of all, part of the story is set in a brothel. Then, although my heroine is eventually reunited with her prime love interest, she is involved with someone else when the story begins. I explained earlier how this extends the potential for conflict and character development. The relationship between the villain's wife and her toy boy lover is also vital to the plot. But I describe the sexual side of their liaison only once, in a few lines, the first time both characters appear together. First I take the toy boy's viewpoint:

> Barry Francis had always found it easy enough to hide his distaste for the soft and sagging middle-aged female flesh that fell with such ease and regularity into his bed.
>
> Maxine Crane might be no softer or saggier than most—but she was certainly richer. Much richer...

A brief dialogue follows, and then I switch to the alternate point of view.

> ...and why not, thought Maxine in delight, with a virile hunk of 29-year-old male like you beneath me? She sucked in her stomach and ground herself harder against him. God, she loved young men. The smooth, firm hardness of them, the ceaseless appetite, the total abandon.

You see, not a four-letter-word in sight! The purpose of the scene is not to titillate but to reveal exactly how the two participants view each other. Readers discover at once that Barry is an opportunist using his good looks and sexual skills to prey on rich women. Maxine's view of her lover reveals her as besotted and gullible.

In the next paragraph, I continue Maxine's inner dialogue to draw the reader further into the plot:

For a moment she let her concentration wander. Barry turned her on so much she wondered why she had resisted for so long. Not, she thought, that Barry had pushed; he'd been the perfect gentleman. It was she who had ached for him, wanted him from the moment they'd met. Only her paranoia that Julian might find out had held her back. If he ever guessed... Maxine pushed the awful thought from her mind.

From here I jump *immediately* to the next scene. There is no need to describe Maxine taking a shower, giving her lover a final lingering kiss, or saying goodbye. I've achieved everything I wanted to do in this scene:

But later, as she sat behind the wheel of her silver-gray BMW, a flush of sexual contentment still coloring her re-done face, the fear stabbed at her again.

An important thing to remember when writing sex scenes is your own gender perspective and possible shortcomings. Women need to ensure that they describe the sexual coupling in physical as well as emotional terms, while for men the opposite is true.

When I had just started to write, I remember reading a scene aloud to a male friend. I had written from the viewpoint of my hero, who was visiting a thirtysomething woman he had once adored. I had him noticing her glossy hair, glowing eyes and velvety skin; he even referred to her dress and jewelry.

At this point my friend stopped me. A man, he said, would be much more aware of a woman's breasts and legs than her hair, eyes, or what she was wearing!

Whenever I am writing about the male animal response I always keep that lesson in mind.

Reading the kinds of books that are selling now will help you decide how much sex your story needs; you know what you feel comfortable with. And if you're planning on trying to emulate the success of *Fifty Shades of Grey*, you'll just have to stop worrying that Aunt Jillian might cut you out of her will!

Write it, don't tell it

It is possible to talk a story to death. I never talk about my work in progress to anyone but my agent. If you talk too much about a story you risk losing the urgency to write it down. After all, why go to all the trouble of putting it down on paper when it's so much easier to tell it aloud?

Even if you are just running your idea past a friend for feedback, you risk letting a single negative judgment defeat you before you start. After all, that discouraging feedback may have less to do with the story itself than with the way you related it—boringly, repeating facts, jumping back and forth to fill in parts you forgot, and so on. And the judgment of a friend is not always as objective and unbiased as it should be—especially if she has always had a secret yearning to write herself!

I am convinced that one of the biggest mistakes you can make is to talk too soon about your story.

Chapter 10: The Shape-Up

Editing and editors

You've done it! You've typed 'THE END'. Take a bow, you've written your first novel!

Now there is one more task awaiting you. What you have written is the first draft. The next step is revision, or editing. Every writer, no matter how experienced, has to face the task of editing. You can always improve a manuscript, but this process does not have to be daunting. You've done the hard part—got the words on paper. You've managed to plot a story, draw characters, and colour in backgrounds. I promise you that editing is much easier than creating those pages in the first place.

There are two kinds of editing: the editing you do yourself and that done by the publisher's editors if your novel is accepted by a traditional print publisher.

The best way to start editing is to do nothing! Once you have typed 'THE END', I strongly advise you to put your manuscript out of sight for a while and try to forget it.

How long, you ask, is 'a while'?

That depends. It should be long enough to ensure that you come back to read your finished story with a fresh eye. This cooling-off period is vital. It should allow you enough distance from your work to be able to judge it as objectively as possible when next you pick it up.

So, hard as it may be, don't re-read your manuscript at once. Instead, think about your next story, take a holiday, visit friends, do whatever is necessary to keep your hands off those typed sheets that represent the first draft of your first novel. I say, 'typed sheets' as my own experience has taught me that I do a much more effective edit at this stage with a hard copy to read and make notes on. Many others of course edit straight from the screen so you will need to see what works best for you.

Whichever method you choose, it is a good idea to read straight through as quickly as possible. Make a note of awkward passages, artificial-sounding dialogue, or inconsistencies in the plotline and keep right on reading.

This is the only way to get a sense of the pace of your story. Pace hinges on the action and plot twists that keep a reader turning the pages—it's when nothing happens in your story that readers lose interest.

One of the most common errors of novice writers is to be boring. Coming to your work with a fresh eye should make it easier for you to identify those sections of the text that make you glaze over. And you can bet that if you're bored your readers will be too. Fixing the dull bits can be as easy as trimming a too-long passage of description or breaking up a block of narrative with a little dialogue.

What should you look for as you edit?

As a novice writer you may sometimes feel at a loss as to what, apart from the glaring errors, needs changing or improving in your work. Here's a guide to help you check through that first draft.

The opening

First, make sure your opening immediately grabs your readers' interest and plunges them into the heart of the story.

Remember, readers of popular fiction are lured by an interesting character or incident. They want action or intrigue from page 1. If you start with paragraphs of description, you're not meeting those expectations. And it's the opening few lines that will persuade a potential reader to buy your book—or another one.

Check, too, that your first few pages aren't a long, drawn-out preamble. Read them carefully. Are they just a warm up? Does your story really begin somewhere on page 3 or 4? If so, scrap those slow opening pages.

Can the beginning of your story be easily grasped without too much explanation? If, in trying to intrigue, you've been too obscure, you'll only confuse your readers.

I can't stress enough the importance of those first two or three pages. Most writers will tell you they rework their opening pages again and again. Editors haven't time to persevere with manuscripts whose first few pages don't appear to have what it takes to get published. So make sure the beginning of your story is *excellent*. If you are publishing as an indie writer then I do think it very worthwhile to pay for an experienced editor, at least the first time around.

Motivation and conflict

Is the problem facing the main character clear right from the start? Is the motivation credible and strong? Is your heroine in genuine conflict with an equally motivated opponent? (It's to be hoped you've made sure of these points before coming this far!)

Structure

Have you achieved a balance between dramatic peaks and the lulls that allow readers to catch their breath? **Check that the climaxes are spread throughout your story and not all crowded into one section.**

Make sure that every incident develops naturally from the one that went before and isn't merely 'tacked on'.

Cut back on long rambling passages that do nothing to develop the plot. Don't short-change your readers either. **If you've been foreshadowing a particularly dramatic scene make sure you don't skip over it too quickly.** Give it the weight it deserves.

You may have to expand some passages for greater clarity. This could entail adding subtle hints about the approaching crisis or enlarging on some vital element in the background of a secondary character.

Ensure that the time span of your story is also balanced. I once read a novel that had 32 chapters. The first 29 filled in the details of the heroine's life to the age of 30, and the next 30-odd years were covered in just three chapters! I was left with the impression that the writer was either bored and desperate to finish or running dangerously close to a publishing deadline.

Action

As you read through your first draft, make sure your heroine is *active*. It's her story you are telling, so she, not the minor characters, should be driving the action. **It's your heroine who makes things happen.**

Have you skirted the 'big scene' by using narrative instead? Remember the rule: show, don't tell.

Check your scenes to make sure they aren't static. Each should give a little more insight into your characters and further develop the storyline. If it doesn't, ask yourself if you really need the scene at all.

Characters

Is your heroine introduced near the beginning of the story? Is she a sympathetic character with whom readers can identify? Does she act consistently?

Your heroine will be more credible if she isn't surrounded by cardboard characters. Have you developed a villain and lesser characters who also have complexity and depth?

Make sure that minor characters are established strongly enough—through description of appearance, habits, the things they do, their manner of speech—so that when they reappear your readers will remember who they are. **Don't forget the 'rule of three' for fixing a character in the reader's mind.**

Avoid stereotypes. Strive for freshness and originality even with minor characters.

Make sure your characters do not all speak with the same voice—that is, that they are not all of the same type. Readers will get confused if you fill your story with young, good-looking, university-educated careerists. Even if characters share a common background, give them distinctive traits and habits. Your aim is to create individuals.

Names

Check the names you've allotted to your characters. Are they too similar? Do too many start with the same initial? Having a Claire, a Catherine and a Cindy can lead to confusion. Have you chosen soft-sounding names for your heroine? Do surnames and first names go well together? Are any foreign names easy enough for English-speaking readers to mentally pronounce?

Have you repeated a character's name too often in a short space? Remember, for variety, to use pronouns.

Setting

Have you made clear where conversations or meetings between characters are taking place? *You* know they're in the kitchen; make sure your readers do too.

It takes just a passing reference to 'place' your characters. The first example below locates the scene with a minimum of fuss. In the second, the scene is left hanging:

He was ready for a showdown the moment he stormed into the house. This time she wasn't going to get off the hook.

He found her in the kitchen.

'I'm not going to let this go on, Louise! We're going to talk about Henry now.'

She gave him that familiar look of bored insolence. 'Jealousy is such a juvenile emotion, Paul.'

Versus:

He was ready for a showdown the moment he stormed into the house. This time she wasn't going to get off the hook.

'I'm not going to let this go on, Louise! We're going to talk about Henry now.'

She gave him that familiar look of bored insolence. 'Jealousy is such a juvenile emotion, Paul.'

Will your readers 'see' the settings you see? Can they also hear, touch, perhaps even smell them? Is the time of day important? Be specific but sparing with your details. Use only those that enhance the atmosphere or tell something about the characters.

For example, if you set a scene in a garden, instead of referring merely to 'trees' and 'flowers' you might describe 'the dense conifers that her great-grandfather had planted', or 'the scent of jasmine that always reminded Diana of summers when she was a child'. Such details add depth and colour to your story by telling more about the characters and their background.

Take care, too, not to set too many scenes in the same place. For variety, change the location or background regularly.

Dialogue

Is there enough dialogue to break up the narration? Do you have too many long, unwieldy speeches? Have you used tag lines for variety?

Is the dialogue appropriate to the character speaking it? Have you made the speech as natural as possible?

To check that your dialogue is 'speakable', read it aloud. Remember that people say: 'I'll', instead of 'I will', or 'she's' instead of 'she is'. Keep an ear out for the places where such contractions are needed.

Have you repeated yourself in dialogue? Does one character tell another things the reader already knows? If this is necessary to the plot, avoid repetition with a brief narrative summary.

'What happened?' she asked.

In a hushed voice he told her what he'd found out.

Viewpoint

Make sure you haven't changed viewpoint within a paragraph. Also check that the viewpoint character knows only what it is possible for her to know; that she isn't, for instance, telling the reader what another character is thinking or feeling.

Remember the importance of using your viewpoint character's inner thoughts to tell your story and give it greater emotional depth. How a character thinks can be much more revealing—and shocking!—than what she says or does. Thoughts give insight into the character's personality.

If you are using multiple viewpoints, have you established this for the reader early enough in the story? Balance is important, too. Check that the various viewpoint characters are brought regularly into the story so that readers don't forget who they are.

Transitions

Do you move too abruptly or awkwardly from scene to scene? Are there places where you need to cut back on overly long transitions? Remember, there is no need to describe what is *implicit* in a scene. If a character is getting out of bed, you don't have to spell out everything she does before she leaves the house.

Exposition

Check for faulty exposition. Have you introduced a character and forgotten to give even the barest description? Have you omitted to ascribe traits or skills she will need later in the story? Do over-long sections of exposition bog your story down? You can avoid this by weaving the exposition gradually into the action or dialogue.

Check all your facts. If a character has blue eyes in Chapter 2, make sure they're not suddenly grey in Chapter 7! If you mention the Sydney Opera House, had it been built at the time of your story? Are you sure how long it takes to travel by train from Los Angeles to Kansas City?

Clichés

Don't worry if a few of these appear when you are in the first flow of writing. Just be aware that in the editing process you will have to be ruthless in getting rid of them. Instead of 'he was tall, dark and handsome', try 'he was above average height with dark, unruly hair and the sort of strong, clean-cut features that spelt masculine in capital letters'. Clichés really grate with editors. The odd one or two can be forgiven but if there are too many in your writing an editor won't bother reading far enough to be impressed by your terrific plot.

Sub-plots

Are these knitted into the main plot or merely tacked on to pad out the story? Have you resolved your sub-plots before the final crisis in the main storyline? Do your sub-plots have all the action and dramatic tension of the main plot?

Flashbacks

Are you sure they have a purpose? Remember that too many flashbacks, if not handled with skill, can confuse your readers. Decide if they are really necessary or if the information they provide can be imparted by some other means.

Coincidences and acts of God

Have you relied too heavily on coincidence to dig you out of plot problems? If you stretch credibility too far, your readers will refuse to go on suspending their disbelief and throw your book away in disgust. It takes hard thinking to come up with plausible solutions that don't depend on flukes or miracles.

Endings

Is the solution to the heroine's problem too predictable? Could it have been reached much earlier in the story? Again, have you relied too much on coincidence or good luck to bring about the ending?

Does your story end on a positive or upbeat note with all loose ends logically tied? Have you avoided anticlimax and too much explanation after the final crisis?

Copy editing

Now that you've made sure the structure of your novel is sound, you should copy edit your manuscript. This entails checking the nitty-gritty of grammar, spelling, punctuation, and so on. This is also the time for cutting out repetitions and superfluous text.

The words most likely to be superfluous are adjectives and adverbs. Look for errors like 'she wept tearfully', 'he shouted loudly'. Don't use three adjectives where one conveys the picture just as well.

Be ruthless in cutting out words like 'just', 'well', 'really' and in over-using 'and', 'but' or 'then'.

Avoid the continuous tenses, which combine the verb 'to be' with a participle. Instead of writing 'she was laughing', or 'he was shouting', for example, use 'she laughed', 'he shouted'.

Break over-long sentences into shorter ones. Look at this unwieldy example:

> *Clutching the drink he had given her, she explored the room and saw on the mantelpiece a silver-framed photograph that showed Mark standing in front of the Randolph Hotel with a tall, fine-featured blonde.*

It works much better like this:

> *Clutching the drink he had given her, she explored the room. On the mantelpiece she saw a silver-framed photograph of Mark and a tall, fine-featured blonde standing outside the Randolph Hotel.*

If you use an unusual word, don't repeat it within the next few pages. It will be too obtrusive. The same goes for using similar expressions or similar tag lines too close together.

Don't overuse conspicuous attributives such as 'barked', 'growled', 'bellowed', and so on. In nearly every case the dialogue itself should indicate how words are spoken.

Don't expect the publisher's or a freelance editor to correct your grammar if your computer program has missed something. If you're shaky on the rules, buy a good grammar guide.

Vary your vocabulary by using the thesaurus function and check that your spell check is accurate for the word in context.

It may come as a surprise to you that writers also have to consider the music of language. The way words and phrases are put together can jar or sound pleasing to the inner ear. Be aware of the natural rhythms of language, and choose words and sentence patterns that give your writing flow and resonance. Too many short, sharp sentences can sound as bad as too many over-long ones. With practice, you will soon learn how to use rhythm for dramatic effect. Consider this description of a fight from *Never Forget Me*:

> The knife flashed. Chris was quick, but not quick enough. A line of crimson immediately sprang up along his shirt sleeve. He grunted, staggered, and his

opponent saw his chance…

This is a dramatic scene and the short, choppy sentences contribute to the sense of action and suspense.

A couple of paragraphs later, the fight over, I change rhythm again.

> Seconds later, as the man's groans grew softer, Chris knelt down beside him and pulled off the balaclava that covered his face.

I could have written:

> *Seconds later the man's groans grew softer. Chris knelt down beside him. He pulled off the balaclava that covered his face.*

But now, with the fight over, the quick, clipped sentences sound awkward. By changing the rhythm I also add to the suspense, as the reader should now be dying to know the identity of the masked man.

The way you set out your paragraphs and sentences can also add impact. Here is another example from *Never Forget Me*:

> Dave Arnell felt his whole body stiffen with shock.
>
> Holy Jesus…
>
> He read the words again. And again.
>
> It couldn't be… It just couldn't be true…

Here I've chopped the passage up into four one-line paragraphs to underline my character's sense of shock. Look how the effect of the third line changes if I substitute: 'He read the words again and again.' As well, the use of the ellipses (…) gives the impression of a man so overwhelmed he finds it difficult to complete a thought.

By trying different ways of punctuating and setting out your scenes you can work out how to achieve the greatest impact.

Editors

As an indie publisher you can choose to do all your own editing or, as I noted earlier, pay for the services of a freelance editor. For those who might be picked up by a traditional publishing house, your manuscript will be handed to an in-house editor who will certainly have further suggestions for improvements.

Ideally, an editor should clarify your prose, point out places where the plot may need tightening, identify problems with credibility and motivation, suggest where to cut and where to expand. Editors may tell you, for example, that you have introduced too many characters too quickly in Chapter 1, or that the tycoon's speech in the confrontation scene needs cutting, or that the murder on page 70 should be foreshadowed in an earlier chapter. This sort of feedback is invaluable in helping you tighten your story and make it more appealing to readers.

What an editor shouldn't do is change the essential voice of your writing or alter anything that doesn't need improving.

When your instincts tell you that something fundamental to your writing has been changed, don't be afraid to speak out. Remember, editors are not writers. They do not face the terror of the blank page. They are employed to fine tune the words that others have toiled to put on that page.

Your editor is responsible for making your manuscript correct in all its details. She may point out that on page 22 Miriam says she hates champagne yet on page 36 she is raising her glass at a party! But it *isn't* the editor's job to check all the fine points of your research, nor to fix a manuscript full of sloppy errors where you might have relied too much on Spellcheck and its occasional incorrect calls.

If you do choose to offer your manuscript to an agent or traditional publishing house, remember you will increase your chances of being published by presenting a clean, professional-looking manuscript that you have already done your very best to pull into shape.

Publishers usually work to strict deadlines, so in most cases you'll have only a few weeks to complete the editing process. After you and the editor have carried out all the improvements you both agree are necessary, the corrected manuscript will be sent to the typesetters.

A few weeks—or months—later, it will be returned to you as page proofs. These are the unbound typeset pages of your work, set out as they will appear in the finished book.

You should check these very carefully for printer's errors. At this stage, too, confronted with fresh, unmarked text, you will almost certainly see other ways to improve your work.

If, as an Indie writer, you employ an editor, it is still up to you to do a thorough check of the final edited draft before uploading.

Titles

When should you think about titles? Before you start? Or after you finish?

It doesn't really matter, but I find myself trying out possibilities at the same time as I am developing my plot. Having a title I like helps to give me a sense of the reality of my next story.

The title of my first book is shown in the contract as *Falls the Shadow*. I took it from the T.S. Elliot line: 'Between the idea and the reality falls the shadow'. At the last moment, my publishers informed me that a book with the same title was being published by a well-known American writer in the same month as mine. Even though there is no copyright on title, it obviously didn't make sense to confuse readers with two identically named novels. I was given a very short time to come up with an alternative and after churning over dozens of possibilities I decided on *Shadows of Power.* It suggested the intrigue and danger of my story and everyone liked it

However as you will know by now that first book eventually became '*Indecent Ambition*' in further editions. Clearly I like that title the best!

The Bible and Shakespeare have already been heavily mined for titles, but you may find an interesting and original title in a slightly less famous work. Perhaps the setting, mood and central characters of your story will stir your imagination. It can help to make a list of key words that pertain to your story and see what you can develop from those.

Sometimes titles tell exactly what the story is about: *The Husband's Secret.* Sometimes they intrigue by their obscurity: *The Light Between Oceans.*

If you're really stumped, a working title is all that is necessary until you come up with something better—and of course you can always brainstorm with your editor or friends.

Choosing the right title isn't easy, and not even the experts can say what works. Look what happened to a story called simply *The Thorn Birds*!

Blurbs/Book Descriptions

The blurb/book description is the short outline of the plot, written to hook your potential reader.

There is quite an art to capturing the essence of your story this way and it takes a bit of practice. Again, it helps to read the blurb on other successful works of popular fiction.

Another good way to test your storyline is by trying to write a blurb for it even before you start work. If you find it difficult to make the idea sound interesting and exciting in précis form, maybe the story needs more thinking through.

Remember, until you become a 'name' author, it's the title, cover, opening paragraphs and blurb that will do most to sell your work. Writing an intriguing blurb is one of the most important ways to grab a reader's interest.

About eBooks and doing it yourself

Most authors use Microsoft Word as their writing tool, some use OpenOffice, some Libre Office. Some use Scrivener, Atlantis, Pages, Vellum… The list goes on.

Most authors also have limited ability using Word and so a group of writers created Draft2Digital (https://www.draft2digital.com/) for this reason. I use it and can recommend this service. You will need to join up and take care of matters such as tax IDs etc. before you begin. Once that is done, start with a good clean copy of your story in .doc or .docx format, and a suitable eBook cover. Whatever program you use, if it can save your document as a .doc or .docx, you're all set to go.

Upload both the document and cover files to Draft2Digital. The process is relatively straight forward if you take your time and read the screen carefully.

The Word document will be converted to an .epub file and a .mobi file. Always check that the .epub file looks ok before you hit the publish button. There are apps for that you'll be pleased to know! You may need to alter the Word file and upload again, time and again, until you like what you see.

You can use Draft2Digital to distribute to many eBook retailers including Apple and Kobo, but you will need to do Amazon Kindle Direct Publishing (KDP) https://kdp.amazon.com yourself and here you use the .mobi file created at Draft2Digital for uploading to Amazon KDP. Again with KDP, it's a case of registering and completing the tax information first.

Amazon is by far the biggest eBook retailer, but note, that if you want to enroll your book in KDP Select, it must be exclusive to Amazon KDP. *You cannot sell it elsewhere.* If all these terms are unfamiliar to you, you'll find more detailed information by researching on line.

The indie highway contains a few steep learning curves, but once all aspects of do-it-yourself authorship are mastered, you will find it gets easier with practice.

There are also writers' forums such as the KDP community, KBoards Writers Café, with experienced indie members who are always willing to help a struggling newbie.

Covers

A good cover will grab a prospective reader as they trawl through the thousands of eBooks on offer at various stores.

Go On Write (http://www.goonwrite.com/) offers plenty of reasonably priced eBook covers for most genres or you can do it yourself if you are competent enough with graphic design. . Remember though that too much detail can get lost in the small thumbnail that readers will first see.

Again, it's a matter of research. There are plenty of how-to sites on the internet.

You cannot upload an eBook without a cover. The more professional a cover, the more interest a reader will take

Marketing

Again, research and beware. There are plenty of websites eager to take your money. Writers' forums can be invaluable.

Create your own website and/or Facebook page. You can always place links to your own website/Facebook page in your author bio and in your email signature.

Paperbacks

KDP now offers Kindle books as paperbacks which is a great option for those readers who still prefer a 'real' book.

Fortunately Draft2Digital can also create the paperback interior from your .doc or .docx file.

You will need to research paperback covers—they are not as straightforward as eBook covers. For an extra fee, Go On Write will create a paperback cover from the eBook cover purchased.

Createspace (https://www.createspace.com/) is an Amazon owned DIY company. You can use their Word templates IF you are competent using Word and understand headers and footers etc. Creating a paperback from your eBook file can be a very steep learning curve and fraught with frustrations for the unsuspecting.

I admit to outsourcing my paperbacks. I want to save my energy for writing!

Creating a Draft2Digital Word file

A few hints

- Never use the Tab button. Forget it ever existed!

- Use Times New Roman 12 as your default font. Anyone reading your story on an electronic device can often change the font to suit themselves anyway.

- Using Styles keeps your document consistent with fonts, font sizes, margins etc., and allows a 'cleaner' conversion to eBook format. The following webpage may be of help: http://www.word-tips.com/microsoft-word-styles/

- Modify your Normal paragraph to include a first line indent of 0.2". To modify a style, go to the Styles tab, *right* click on Normal and Modify/Format/Paragraph.

- Use Heading 1 for Chapters and modify the Heading 1 style to 'start on a new page', found in Format/Paragraph/Line & Page Breaks. Draft2Digital's converter will use your Heading 1 style to recognize chapters and will create your table of contents for you.

- Use Normal (modified with first line indent) for text paragraphs.

- To denote a sequence break, put in 3 return/enters. When Draft2Digital's converter recognizes 3 return/enters, it puts in a space.

- Remember to include your author biography or About the Author page (with links to your website and/or Facebook) at the end of the story, or create a biography using Draft2Digital's facility.

This site may also be invaluable to you: https://janefriedman.com/how-to-publish-an-ebook/?platform=hootsuite

Chapter 11: The Magic Moment

You did it!

At last.

Either your book has been through the traditional publishing mill and the box of books has arrived, or you are an indie publisher, your book is available at various retailers and you have the proof copy of your paperback in your hands.

Suddenly you realize that you can now count yourself among the elite—a *published author*! You'll get misty-eyed as you think of your famous predecessors—Shakespeare! Steinbeck! Balzac!—and you'll bless the day that Caxton developed the printing press just so you could experience your own unique moment of glory.

And it *is* a terrific feeling to know that the story you wove in solitude from your imagination is now going to be read by people you will probably never know but who are going to be thrilled and entertained by the characters and events you describe. (And hopefully write you a glowing review!)

I began this book by promising to offer you motivation, confidence and practical advice. From this point onwards only your own determined efforts will reveal whether you possess that other necessary ingredient: talent.

Yet if you never make an attempt at writing that novel you've dreamed of for so long, how will you ever know if you have what it takes to be a published author?

When I began I was no surer than you are now. Since then I have not only written eight successful novels and two non-fiction works, but have surprised myself by writing screenplays, short stories and feature articles! I've appeared on many leading television programs and been invited to speak at numerous writer's festivals. My career has been a dream come true.

In this book, I haven't glossed over the fact that discipline, determination and sacrifice are all part of the journey ahead of you. But always bear in mind that the biggest names in the business had to start just as you are starting now. Be confident, stay focused, use the tools you find helpful in this book and you too may find the wonderful joy of tapping the source of creativity inside you. I can assure you that the effort is well and truly worth it.

So don't put it off a moment longer.

Start that novel today.

And the very best of luck!

About The Author

Jennifer Bacia's first novel *Indecent Ambition,* was bought for a record-breaking advance and became an international best-seller. The novel was a lead title in the UK, Book of the Month for Book Club and the film rights were sold. *Cosmopolitan* magazine bought extract rights, the audio rights were sold and the novel was translated into German, Greek, Polish and Swedish.

Since then, Jennifer has published seven more novels that have also made the bestseller lists. Her many short stories have been published in leading magazines, and she has written screenplays and had her own newspaper and magazine columns Her non-fiction works include a guide to popular fiction writing : *Bestseller! Writing Fiction that Sells.* She was invited to establish the first creative writing course at Bond University.

Jennifer's name is pronounced 'batcher' and is of Polish/Italian origin.

For more information, you can visit her website:

http://www.jenniferbacia.net

And go to her Facebook page:

https://www.facebook.com/jenniferbacia.net/

Please note that some of Jennifer's original print published titles have been changed in digital format.

Indecent Ambition: original title 'Shadows of Power'

Whisper her Name: original title 'Angel of Honor'

A Very Public Scandal: original title 'Mask of Paradise'

Never Forget Me: 'Whisper from the Gods'

One Door Closes: 'Table for Three'

www.ingramcontent.com/pod-product-compliance
Lightning Source LLC
Chambersburg PA
CBHW050348280326
41933CB00010BA/1376